D0570883

NATIVE AMERICAN MYTHS

NATIVE AMERICAN MYTHS

DIANA FERGUSON

CONSULTANT: COLIN TAYLOR

COLLINS & BROWN

First published in Great Britain in 2001 by
Collins & Brown Limited
64 Brewery Road
London N7 9NT

A member of Chrysalis Books plc

British Library Cataloguing-in-Publication Data: A catalogue record for this book is available from the British Library

ISBN: 1-85585-824-X

2 3 4 5 6 7 8 9

Consultant: Colin Taylor
Project Editor: Jane Ellis
Editor: Jean Coppendale
Designer: Emily Cook
Picture Researchers: Simon Brockbank, Jessica Cowie
Photographers: Ben Connor, Colin Taylor
Indexer: David Lee
Map Artwork: John Gilkes

Color reproduction by: Global Colour Limited, Malaysia
Printed by: Dai Nippon Printing Co Limited, Hong Kong

Contents

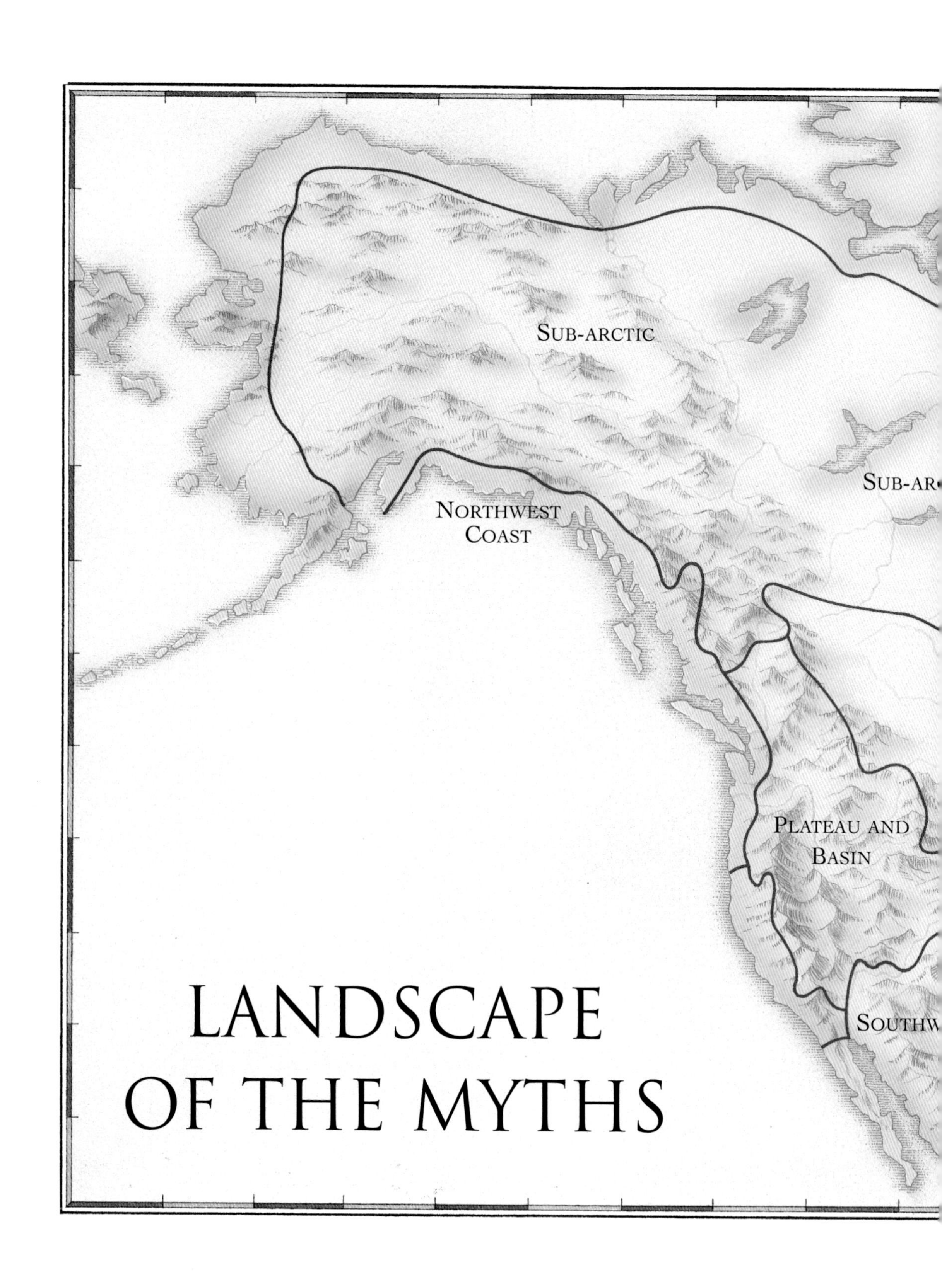

LANDSCAPE OF THE MYTHS

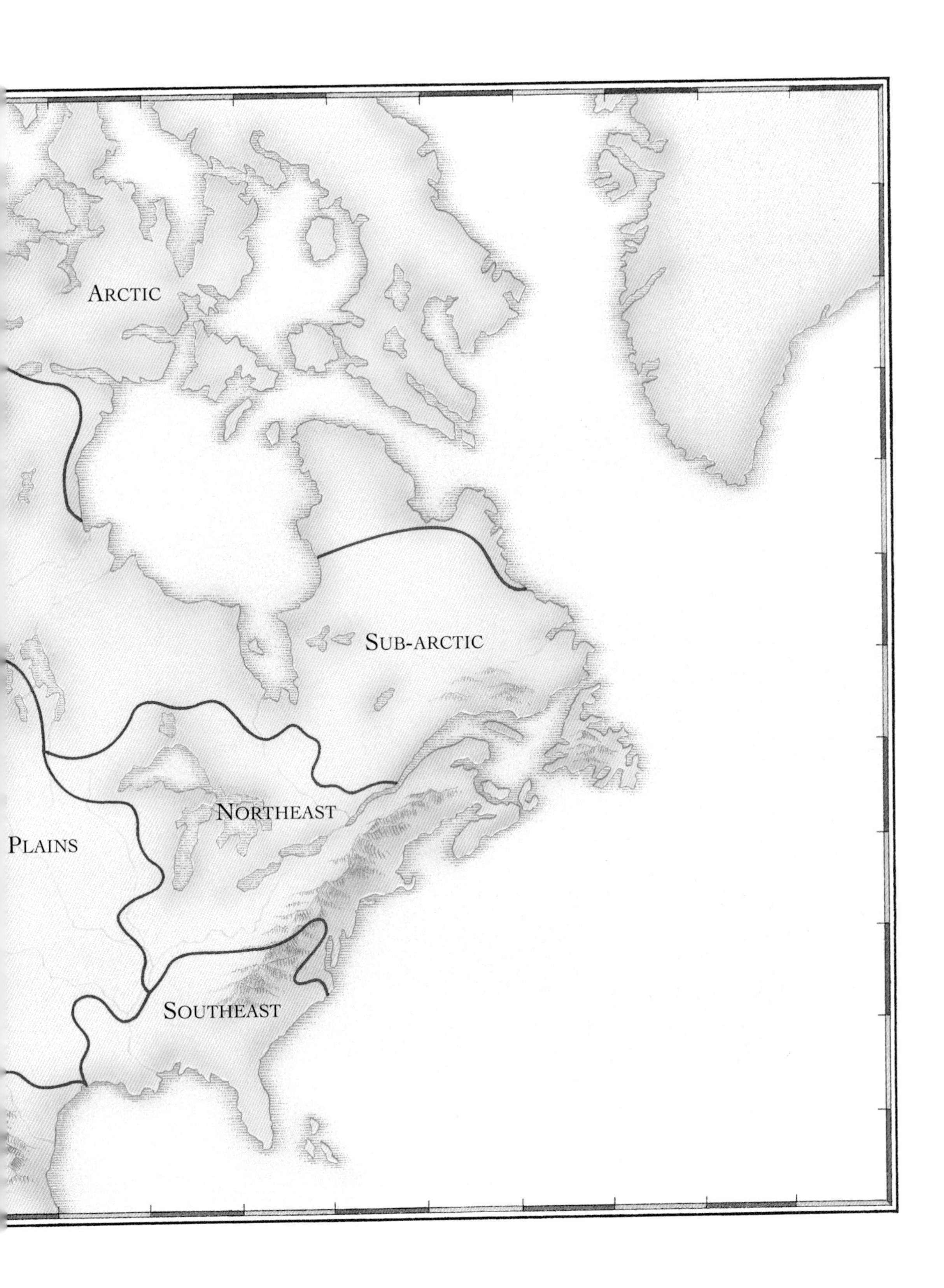

Arctic
Sub-arctic
Northeast
Plains
Southeast

INTRODUCTION

During the Earth's long history, periods of glaciation have covered large tracts of the planet in massive sheets of ice, solidifying vast quantitites of water and causing sea levels to drop. The significance of this, in historical terms, is that it determined the identity of the first North Americans.

In the prolonged big freezes which occurred between 75,000 and 45,000 BCE, and again between 25,000 and 14,000 BCE, glaciation exposed the territory normally covered by the waters of the Bering Strait which separates Asia and North America, and created a land-bridge – now known as Beringia – connecting the two continents. It was across Beringia that prehistoric hunters from Asia were thought to have migrated at the end of the last Ice Age around 11,000 years ago, moving eastwards following the herds – mammoth, bison, caribou, wild horse, reindeer – to enter North America and become its first human inhabitants. However, more recent evidence, including the discovery of stone tools in Chile dating back some 33,000 years, and prehistoric skulls which are quite distinct from those of modern Native Americans, have led scientists to question the earlier theory.

Thousands of years later, Christopher Columbus was to encounter their descendants. Mistaking the continent at which he had arrived for the East Indies, he called its inhabitants *Indios*. The name stuck: ever since then, the first peoples of North America have been known as 'Indians'.

That, at any rate, is the scientific explanation. Native American mythic tradition tells another story. The Indians, it maintains, were not migrants from another place who came to inhabit North America – they have always been there, ever since the day Coyote placed them on the Earth, or Raven released them from the clam shell in which he found them.

TERRITORIES AND TALES

Ethnologists divide North American Indians, or Native Americans as many prefer to call them, into different groups according to language and geographical area. Geographical divisions are particularly relevant to mythology, for it is out of peoples' observations of their environment and their mystical relationship with the world around them that their gods and spirits and stories grew. Although many universal themes thread through the web of Native American mythology – themes common to humankind in general – there is often a qualitative difference of mood in the myths of individual regions, reflecting the particular environments that gave them birth, be they ocean shore, lakeland, woodland, or arid desert.

THE FAR NORTH

The Arctic is the northernmost of these geographical regions. The inhabitants of this harsh environment are descendants of the Eskimo-Aleuts who are estimated to have crossed the Bering Strait around 10,000 years ago, and who evolved into three linguistic groups: the Aleut, the Yupik, and the Inuit-Inupiaq.

The Eskimo in his igloo is the stereotypical image of the indigenous Arctic dweller. Over the last 30 years, however, the term 'Inuit' has come to replace the generic 'Eskimo', which is said to be derived from a derogatory Algonquian term meaning 'raw meat eater'. As for the igloo, (from the Inuit-Inupiaq *igdlu*), this was not the general form of habitation, as the stereotype suggests, but was restricted mainly to the Central Arctic. More common forms of dwelling were the *karmak*, a semi-subterranean chamber with a turf-covered roof, and the *tupik*, a caribou or sealskin tent for the summer months when life was partly nomadic.

Of all Native Americans, the inhabitants of the Arctic retain perhaps the strongest facial

resemblance to their Mongolian ancestors. Like the unforgiving environment in which they live, their myths are stark in character, with none of the lyrical mysticism of, say, Navajo tales or those from the Great Lakes region. A brutal, incestuous rape is the deed which sets the Sun on its course in the sky (see page 77); in contrast to European tradition, this Sun is female like the Sun in Japanese myth, hinting at ancient Inuit connections with aboriginal Asia. Similarly, the sea creatures – the seal, the walrus, and the whale – are the result of a dismemberment of a daughter by her father (see page 86).

Immediately to the south of the Arctic lies the Sub-Arctic region, a vast and sparsely populated territory spanning the entire continent from west to east, and home to peoples speaking Algonquian and Athapaskan languages such as the Cree and the Chippewyan. Life in this often hostile territory was precarious and, as elsewhere, the mythology of the region served to make sense of the world and to reassure the inhabitants that, through correct action and the observance of taboos, they could have at least some influence over the forces of nature.

BY THE BIG WATER

Running alongside and to the southwest of the Sub-Arctic is the ribbon territory classified as the Northwest Coast region. Fronting the Pacific, backed by cedar forests, and with a heavily indented coastline with numerous inlets, this is a land that has an intimate relationship with the sea. Its inhabitants are whalers and fishermen, and its myths are imbued with a powerful sense of place. One has only to read them to hear the call of the seabirds and the crash of the waves, or see, in the mind's eye, the mist rolling in and the face of the Sky Spirit, wings outspread, in the gathering clouds. The originators of these wonderful stories include the Tlingit, Haida, Tsimshian, Kwakiutl, Nootka and Makah.

Moving directly south, one arrives at another region with a long Pacific coastline – California. According to archeological evidence, there were humans living here more than 20,000 years ago. They survived by hunting, gathering and fishing. Such was the natural bounty of the area that it was unnecessary to grow crops or to migrate with the herds, and life was generally settled and peaceful. The Hokan and Penutian language groups dominated the area, and tribes included the Shasta, Pomo and Miwok.

THE GREAT HINTERLAND

To the east and southeast of the Northwest Coast area is the Plateau and Basin region. Stretching from the middle of British Columbia to northern Arizona and New Mexico, it takes in a wide range of climate and terrain, from mountain ranges and great riverways iin the north to open scrubland in the south. Such geographical diversity naturally produced many diverse cultures. Like all Native Americans, however, they shared a common belief in the sacredness of all natural things, animate and inanimate – earth, water, plants, animals, and so on. Tribes of the Plateau include the Kalispel, Flathead, and Nez Percé. In the Great Basin lived the Bannock and Shosone, and the Paviotso, Paiute and Ute.

East of the Plateau and Basin we come to the heartland of Native America. This is the land that everyone knows from countless Westerns – the land of cowboys and Indians, covered wagons, *tipis* and mounted warriors, proud chiefs with feather headdresses, buffalo and cattle, vast horizons and limitless skies. It is the region known as the Great Plains. The names of the Plains Indians read like a roll call from the Old West, for this is the territory of the Sioux, Comanche, Blackfeet, Crow, Pawnee, Cheyenne and other tribes.

Like the Eskimo and his igloo, the Plains Indian and his horse seem an inseparable partnership and one which, we are led to believe, always existed. The image, however, is slightly misleading since prior to the coming of the Spanish in the sixteenth century, the Indians had no horses, the indigenous wild animal having died out. Up until this time, dogs were the only domesticated beasts of burden, and were used to pull the *travois*, a type of A-framed sledge on which possessions could be transported – an essential requirement in the lives of these nomadic peoples. Hunting the buffalo, which provided food, clothing and other prerequisites of life, was done on foot.

For the Plains Indians of the New World, the introduction of the horse as a means of transport was a hugely significant innovation, as it was for the early Indo-European horsemen of the Old World. When the Indians acquired the animal from the Spanish in the south, it transformed their lives. They now had a mobility they had never enjoyed before, along with the advantage of speed; they could transport heavier loads, and so their *tipis* – portable conical structures of poles and hide which facilitated a nomadic lifestyle – could be larger; and they changed their style of hunting, from stampeding the buffalo herds into V-shaped enclosures to shooting them on the hoof. (Not all Plains Indians used the *tipi*; some tribes, such as the Mandan, lived in dome-shaped, earth-shaped lodges, in semi-permanent settlements.)

With no access to the sea and with its wide, open skies, it is natural that the Plains landscape engendered a profound reverence for the sky. Indeed, the blue of the heavens was in itself sacred for, in its intense infinity, it embodied the creative force of the universe, known variously by such names as Wakan Tanka and Tirawa.

THE GREAT LAKES

Moving eastwards from the Great Plains, one arrives at the Northeast region. This vast area runs from the Great Lakes in the north and west to the Atlantic coast in the east and North Carolina and Virginia in the south. The two main linguistic groups are the Algonquian, which includes such tribes as the Micmac, Chippewa (also known as the Ojibwa), Menominee, and Shawnee; and the Iroquois, including the Mohawk, Seneca, Huron and Susquehannock. These Northeast tribes lived by gathering and farming, hunting and fishing.

It was one such group – the Wampanoag of southern Massachusetts – who played a small but significant role in the history of white America. On 26 December 1620, a group of around 100 emigrants from England, who came to be known as 'Pilgrims' because of their quest for religious freedom, sailed across Cape Cod Bay in their ship, the *Mayflower*, and landed at a place called Plymouth. After a very hard winter, in which half of their number died through sickness, lack of food, difficult weather, and overwork, they were approached by local Indians who showed them how to catch and use a type of herring as fertilizer and how to grow indigenous food plants – corn, pumpkins and beans. That autumn, after a successful harvest, the Pilgrims invited the Indians to share in a three-day feast of thanks. Ninety of them joined the white settlers in the celebration, the first of its kind and one which would later become a national American institution: Thanksgiving.

The myths and legends of the Northeast have a distinctive character and often a particular, poignant beauty (see, for example, 'The Boy Who

Ran With the Wolves, page 147, or 'The Wooden Doll', page 151). They have been immortalized, too, in American literature. James Fenimore Cooper's *The Last of the Mohicans*, published in 1826, focuses on the Mohican tribe of what is now northern Vermont, while Henry Wadsworth Longfellow's famous narrative poem *The Song of Hiawatha*, with its sing-song metre inspired by the Finnish epic, the *Kalevala*, is set among the Ojibwa of Lake Superior. Its eponymous hero, son of the West Wind, is a fictional figure of the mythical saviour type, 'founded' according to the poet, 'on a tradition prevalent among the North American Indians, of a personage of miraculous birth, who was sent among them ... to teach them the arts of peace.' The historical Hiawatha – Haion'hwa'tha – was a Mohawk chief and advocate of a League of Nations among the Indians. The Ojibwa legend of Mondawmin (see 'Mondawmin the Corn Spirit', page 122), originally collected by Henry Rowe Schoolcraft (1793–1864), became the basis of Part V of the poem, *Hiawatha's Fasting*.

Deep South

South of the territory of the Algonquians and Iroquois lies the home of the Choctaws, Cherokees, Creeks and Seminoles: the Southeast. Spanning an area extending into Kentucky and Virginia in the north, and bounded by the Mississippi River in the west, the Atlantic Ocean in the east, and the Gulf of Mexico in the south, it is culturally very fragmented and it is difficult to piece together a cohesive picture of the area's history and former inhabitants. There is, however, evidence of human habitation here going back millennia, and signs of Mexican and South American influences. Ancient mound-builders, at work for thousands of years up to about 600 CE, filled the area with their creations – burial mounds and earthworks representing people, animals and birds, such as the extraordinary Serpent Mound which snakes for 0.4 kilometres (¼ mile) across the Ohio landscape.

After the mound-builders came the Mississippian culture, whose most famous achievement was the city of Cahokia, dating from around 1200 CE. Centred around a stepped pyramid-shaped mound reminiscent of Aztec pyramids and broader at its base than the Great Pyramid of Egypt, the city was home to some 30,000 people. Sun worship and some human sacrifice was practised here, as throughout the region. By the time of the Indian wars with the French in the 1730s, this ancient culture – the most developed in North America – had completely vanished.

Worse was to come, however. In the winter of 1838–39, the Cherokees, many of whom were reluctant to leave their ancient homelands despite having agreed to sell them to the United States, were removed by brute force, bribery and deception, to what is now Oklahoma. Around four thousand of them died on the journey, which became known as the Trail of Tears. This, and the massacre at Wounded Knee (29 December, 1890), live on as scars in the memory of the relations between Indian and White Man, and are witness to two irreconcilable and opposing world views.

PUEBLOS AND POLLEN

The ninth and final region into which indigenous North America is divided is the Southwest. This is the land of the Grand Canyon and the desert, extending from Utah and Colorado down through Arizona to Mexico. The earliest inhabitants, during a period lasting several thousand years BCE, were hunter-gatherers; by about 200 BCE, they were replaced by the Hohokam, who were early farmers and whose descendants include the Pima and Papago.

In the north of the region another culture, the Anasazi, flourished from about 900–1300 CE. Expert builders, they constructed houses of stone in the sides of cliffs or beneath rock overhangs, which could be four or five storeys high. The Spanish named the settlements of these cliff-dwellers *pueblos*. Climatic change and roving bands of warlike nomads from the north drove the Anasazi away, to seek safer and more fertile places to live. Their descendants are collectively known as Pueblo Indians: those who migrated towards the Rio Grande are the River Pueblos; others who travelled to the Arizona desert are the Desert Pueblos, and include the Zuni and Hopi. Understandably in such a habitat, snakes and rainmaking are important features of Desert Pueblo mythology and ritual.

The nomads who helped to drive away the pueblo dwellers were Athapaskan-speakers who had left their original homeland in the Sub-Arctic around 1000 CE and gradually moved southwards. Some had settled near the Pueblo Indians who, seeing their lack of interest in agriculture, called them *apaches de nabahu* or 'enemies of the cultivated fields'. Some of these Athapaskans did finally settle down; among them were the tribe who became known as the Navajos, after their Pueblo name. Others, further to the east, stuck to their wild, nomadic ways, but earned a reputation for bravery in war; they were the Apaches.

The myths of the Indians of the Southwest are more than mere stories: they are a repository of cultural values, and still form an important part of ceremonial life. The Navajo, in particular, who absorbed many of their Pueblo neighbours' religious beliefs and ritual practices, have produced myths of a luminous beauty and extraordinary imagery – the gold of the horizon is not mist but a dusting of pollen given

in offering to the Sun; the Sun is not a distant ball of fire but a divine being who crosses the heavens on one of several horses, the colour of his horse determining the colour and mood of the sky. This is language of the soul of the very highest order.

BY WORD OF MOUTH

The tales which follow are but a very small selection – no more than a taster – of the huge number of stories belonging to Native American tradition. Some revel in an earthy humour, some shimmer with beauty and sadness, some simply explain, in the most imaginative ways, 'how things came to be'. Here you will meet that ancient mythological archetype who makes his appearance in legends all around the world – the Trickster. Here, too, is the figure of the Hero who – like his cousins in ancient Greece, Britain and many other localities – goes on his iniatiatory, shamanic quest into the Otherworld. Animals also abound here, as do some specifically Native American supernaturals.

As in many other cultures, these myths come from an oral tradition. They were not written down but passed on from one generation to the next by word of mouth. While a written narrative is different from, and often does not have the compelling power of, the same story told 'live'– perhaps by the fireside in the magical darkness of a winter's night – setting these tales down on paper does help to preserve them for us and for future generations, for they are part of the spiritual heritage of a particular people and enrich the lives of us all.

It is appropriate that the last word on the matter should come from the mouth of a Native American. In the late 1880s, when the Indians had been corralled into reservations and forced to abandon their old way of life, the writer and explorer George Bird Grinnell visited his friend, the Pawnee chief White Eagle, and explained that he wanted to collect the history and stories of the chief's people and put them all down in a book. White Eagle meditated a while, and then replied: 'It is good and it is time. Already the old things are being lost, and those who knew the secrets are many of them dead. If we had known how to write, we would have put all these things down, and they would not have been forgotten, but we could not write, and these stories were handed down from one to another. The old men told their grandchildren, and they told their grandchildren, and so the secrets and the stories and the doings of long ago have been handed down. It may be that they have changed as they passed from father to son, and it is well that they should be put down, so that our children, when they are like the white people, can know what were their fathers' ways.'

A few of their fathers' stories may be found in the pages of this book.

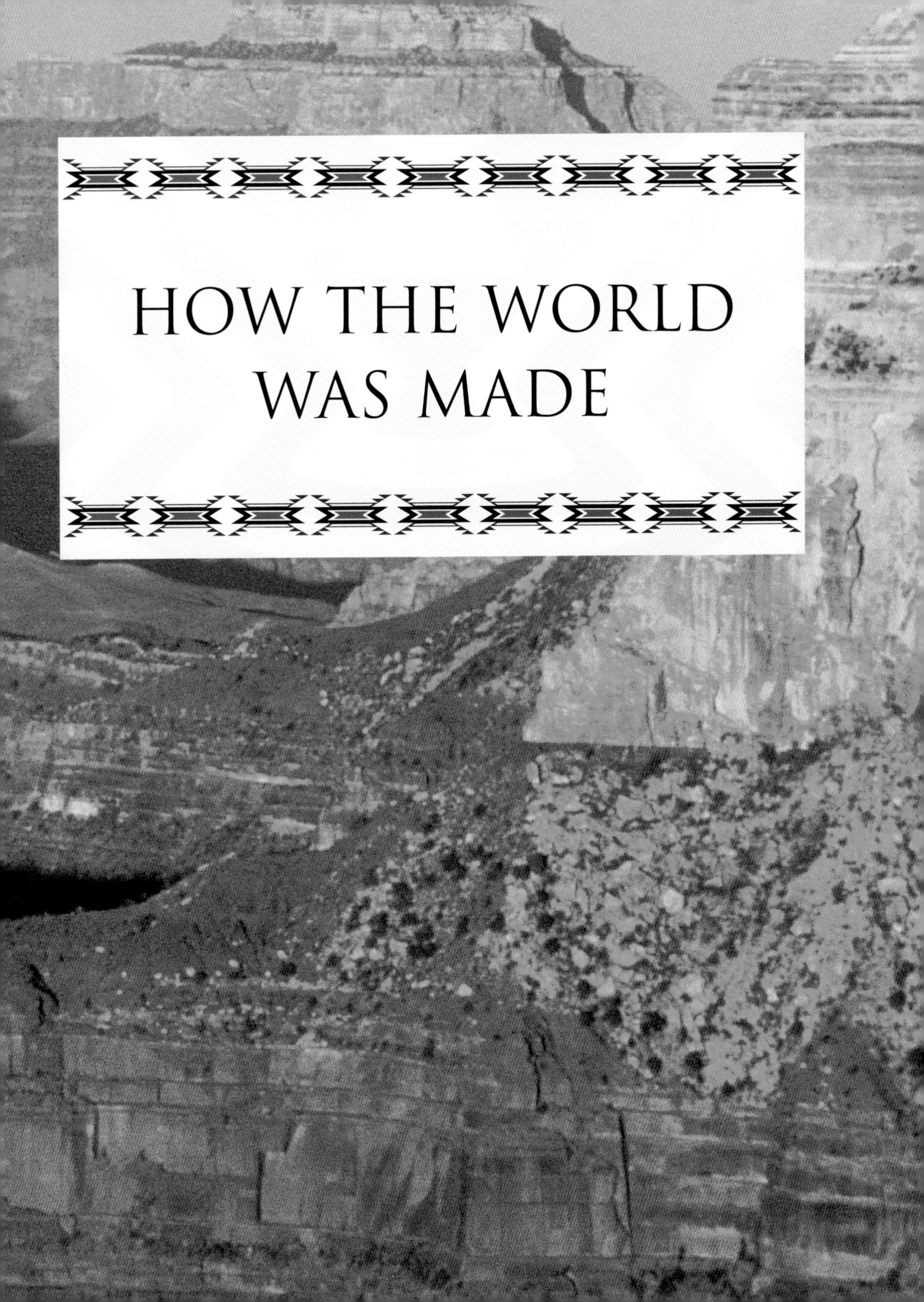

HOW THE WORLD WAS MADE

Tirawa and the Song of the Stars

PAWNEE • PLAINS

THE PRAIRIE GRASSES TOSS and sigh beneath the boundless blue of heaven, and in that infinite blueness is Tirawa. It is he who made the world, long, long ago. Up in the sky-country, Tirawa began the work of creation.

'Go to the east,' he said to Shakaru the Sun and to Big Star, the Morning Star. 'Shakaru shall light the world by day. Big Star shall be a warrior who banishes the darkness.'

'Go to the west,' he said to Pah the Moon and Bright Star, the Evening Star. 'Pah shall light the world by night. Bright Star shall be the mother of all.'

Then he sent the Pole Star to the north and the Star of Death to the south, and stationed a star in each quarter – northeast, southeast, southwest, northwest.

'Stay there,' he said to the four stars, 'and hold up the sky.'

He sent Clouds, Winds, Lightning and Thunder to live with Evening Star, clothing them with buffalo-skin robes and soft moccasins.

When Tirawa commanded, the elements came. The Clouds gathered, the Winds

THE FOUR DIRECTIONS

In many cultures, four is a sacred number which defines the physical structure of the universe. For the Native Americans, its importance can be seen in the symbol for the Morning Star, which consists of four points enclosed within a circle – the four directions, east, south, west, and north, which dissect and are contained by the whole. In 'Tirawa and the Song of the Stars', the Creator deliberately appoints heavenly bodies to take up their respective stations in each of the four directions. (The Morning and Evening Stars which accompany, respectively, the Sun in the east and the Moon in the west are, in reality, both the planet Venus.) Like the *bacab* dwarves of Maya tradition or the dwarves of Norse mythology, all of whom are skybearers, it is the job of the stars of the four directions to support the heavens.

The universe of the Indians of the Southwest also has a four-part structure, but here the division is vertical rather than horizontal. In the Hopi myth, 'Climbing the Ladder of the Worlds' (page 26), there are four successive worlds, stacked one above the other like discs, the present world being the fourth. The Navajo have a similar image, except that four worlds lie beneath the present one, which is the fifth.

If the whole is made up of four equal parts, these must meet at some point. As the traditional storyteller's opening states, 'In the place where north, south, east and west meet ... which is where? At your feet!', this meeting point is in the centre – the fifth direction which mythologists sometimes refer to as the World Navel. It is through their own particular World Navel that the Hopi emerge; this is their ancestral 'place of origin' which allows them rightful claim to the region for it is where they were 'born'. Similar place-of-origin myths are told by the Maya and Incas, who were also Native Americans, living further south.

The reed up which the Hopi climb and which links all the worlds is another important symbol for it equates to the mythological World Tree or *axis mundi* (axis of the world) which is, as it were, the spine or pivot of the universe. In the Sun Dance ceremony (see page 120), the pole at the centre of the lodge also represents this World Tree.

began to blow, and Lightning and Thunder ran wildly among them, crackling and flashing and booming. The Clouds angrily darkened their faces and massed together in vast, billowing banks which covered the sky. Tirawa took a pebble and threw it into their midst. The Clouds drew aside to reveal a vast sheet of water, far, far below.

Then Tirawa armed the stars of the quarters with war-clubs. 'Hit the water with your clubs,' he said. And as they smashed it with their weapons, it parted to reveal the Earth beneath.

'Sing!' Tirawa told them. And they raised their voices in star-song and their singing hummed through the universe and roused the elements to a frenzy. The Clouds turned black. The Winds howled. Thunder raged. Lightning snapped. And such was the ferocity of their combined power that it split the face of the Earth, cracking it open to make valleys and mountains.

'Sing!' said Tirawa again. And this time the song of the stars was a hymn to forest and prairie, a praise-song to all forms of vegetation. When the elements heard it they were once again stirred to fever pitch. They rampaged, they exploded, they wept – and released all their pent-up fury in a downpour of life-giving rain which fed the Earth and made it verdant with trees and grasses.

'Sing!' said Tirawa again. And this time the star-song called into being all the rivers and streams.

'Sing!' said Tirawa. And the star-song awoke all the little seeds sleeping in the Earth, and made them sprout and grow and flower.

Then Morning Star and Evening Star united, and Sun and Moon did, too, and the result of these pairings was a daughter and a son, First Woman and First Man. Tirawa sent them gifts as befitted their roles and the tasks they had to do. The hut and the hearth, the arts of speech and fire making, and seeds and moisture to make them grow – all these things were given to the woman. Weapons and war paint, hunting skills, and knowledge of the names of animals and of the rituals of smoking and sacrifice were given to the man.

First Man became chief of the first people, and when they built their camp they laid it out in the pattern of the stars, in memory of how the world had been created.

HOW THE FIRST PEOPLE WERE MADE

PIMA • SOUTHWEST

THE MASTER OF LIFE HAD BEEN WORKING HARD. He had just finished making the world. He had spread out the land like a giant yellow blanket beneath the searing-blue dome of heaven. He had shaped the *mesas*, the flat-topped hills, gouged out the canyons, and sculpted soaring columns of rock. He had filled the riverbeds with water. He had made the piñon tree and the yucca, the grass and the flowers, the eagle and the turkey, the ant and the bee. All these things were of his own invention, each different in its own way, each perfectly adapted to its place in creation.

The Master of Life had made all these wonders, and now he was tired. He sat down to rest and looked about him. What he had made was good, very good, and he was pleased. And yet, somehow, something was lacking. What could it be?

He sat and thought. The world he had made was teeming with life. There were animals and birds and insects, but in all of creation, there were no beings like himself. That was it! There were no *people* to make creation complete.

So the Master of Life took a lump of clay and pinched and pummelled it into a shape just like himself. He built himself an oven and placed the clay doll inside. Then he went off to gather wood for the fire so that he could bake the little figure until it was just right.

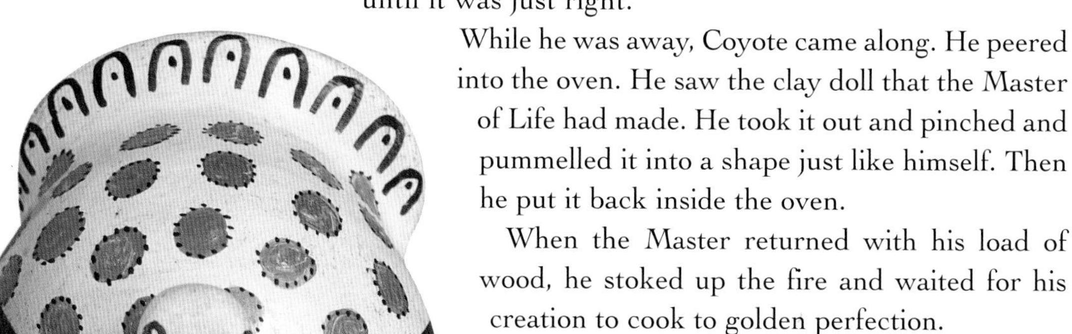

While he was away, Coyote came along. He peered into the oven. He saw the clay doll that the Master of Life had made. He took it out and pinched and pummelled it into a shape just like himself. Then he put it back inside the oven.

When the Master returned with his load of wood, he stoked up the fire and waited for his creation to cook to golden perfection.

'It must be ready now,' he said after a while. So he took out the figure and breathed the breath of life into it.

It stood up on its four legs and wagged its tail and barked.

It was a dog.

'This can't be right!' said the Master of Life. 'I made a creature with two legs, not four. This is your doing, isn't it?' And he scowled at Coyote.

'But he's perfect!' replied Coyote. 'Can't you see? He's exactly like me!'

The Master of Life began all over again. He took another lump of clay and shaped it into a shape just like himself. Then he made another, exactly like the first, to be its companion.

'Hmm,' he thought, 'there is something missing. They don't have what they need to make babies.' So he cut a little slit between the legs of the one, and added a blob of clay between the legs of the other. 'There,' he said to himself. 'That should do it.' And he placed them in the oven to bake.

'Take them out, take them out!' yelled Coyote after a few minutes. 'I can smell them burning.'

So the Master of Life took out the clay figures. But Coyote was lying. They weren't cooked enough. They were underdone, with skin as white as chalk.

'You lied to me!' said the Master of Life. 'Look at them – they are so pale. They do not belong here.' And he breathed the breath of life into them and sent them away, to a land across the sea.

Then he began all over again. But this time, when he bent to take out the figures, Coyote shouted: 'Leave them, leave them! You haven't cooked them enough.' So the Master of Life left them in the oven for so long that by the time he did take them out they were completely overdone, with skin as black as ebony.

'Why do I listen to you?' he said to Coyote. 'Look at them – they are so dark. They do not belong here.' And he breathed the breath of life into them and sent them away, to a land across the sea.

He placed a third pair of clay figures in the oven. But this time he ignored Coyote's meddlesome advice and trusted to his own judgement. As a result, when he removed them from the oven, he saw that they were baked to golden perfection, with skin that glowed like copper.

'Aah!' sighed the Master of Life. 'Just right!' And so they were.

And they have been just right ever since, for these copper-coloured people were the first Pima Indians.

Climbing the Ladder of the Worlds

HOPI • SOUTHWEST

Deep below the Earth, in the first of the four worlds, the first people once lived. Their cave-world was without light: it was black, pitch black, and they had to fumble in the darkness.

As more and more people were born, the cave-world became even more crowded. The people jostled with each other for space. 'Get out of my way – move over!' they shouted at each other. A man could not spit without spattering his neighbour, nor sneeze without spraying those next to him. The odours of breath and sweat and filth filled the stagnant air. It was intolerable, but what could the people do? They had nowhere else to go.

'Ai!' they wailed and wept. 'We cannot breathe, we cannot move, we cannot see. This life is too much for us!' They longed to escape from the first world, to come out of the darkness and into the light.

Beyond the worlds, the spirit beings were watching. They saw the people's distress. Elder Brother and Younger Brother took pity on them. So they made holes in all the roofs of the three lower worlds, and threw seed down into the soil of the first.

One of the seeds took root, and the plant that came from it grew and grew and grew until its top disappeared through the opening in the roof. It was a reed, strong and sturdy enough to take the weight of many men, with joints along its length like the steps on a ladder.

Groping around in the darkness, the people discovered the reed. They felt it and fingered it. What was this strange plant, and where did it lead? So they began to clamber up it, placing one foot then the other on each of the joints – men and women and children, and animals, for they were there too – until they found that they had climbed all the way out of the first world and into the second.

But the second world was subterranean like the first, and just as dark. Fearing that it would not be big enough for all of them, the people who were furthest up the reed-ladder shook it so that all those below them fell off. Then they pulled the reed up through the hole, and left the others to find their own way out of the Earth later.

IN THE SECOND WORLD

All went well for a while in the second world. But then, just as before, the number of people swelled so that in the end this world was, if anything, more crowded than the first. The same old complaints and quarrels were heard. 'Why should you have more room than me – just who do you think you are?' 'That's my place, and you have stolen it!' 'Look where you're going! You've just stepped on my foot!' But of course, no one could look where they were going because it was too dark to see, and so crowded that everyone kept bumping into each other. They longed to escape from the second world, to come out into the light.

So they brought out the reed-ladder which they had been keeping safe all this time. They lifted it up, pushing one end into the soil to steady it and aiming the other through the hole in the roof. And then they began to climb, men, women, children and animals as before, up, up, up into the third world. Again, as they neared the top they shook off those who were slower and further down the ladder, and left them to find their own way out of the Earth.

IN THE THIRD WORLD

Up in the third world, it was still dark for it was underground like the others. But here life was much better. Elder Brother and Younger Brother gave the people fire so that they could light torches to see their way. The men built huts of mud for their families and *kivas*, underground chambers in which to hold their sacred ceremonies. Here, the holy men made their preparations and then they and other chosen men, dressed as *kachinas* – benign spirits – with feathered masks and kilts and rattles, danced through the villages, the *pueblos*, to bring good luck to all the people.

But then bad times came. It all started among the women. They took to dancing, and they danced and danced like souls possessed. They were unable to stop. They danced in the *kivas* that belonged to the men. They danced when they should have been performing their wifely duties – cooking and cleaning and caring for their families.

They lay down only to sleep. As soon as they were rested they were up again, shaking their rattles and stamping their feet and swaying their hips in rhythm. 'Go away! Can't you see we are busy?' they cried to their husbands when they tried to take them home. In the pulsating throng, the men could not tell whose wife was whose and they had to become mothers to the babies, only taking them to the women when they needed feeding. They longed to escape from the third world, to come out into the light.

So, as they had done twice before, they brought out the reed-ladder, fixing one end in the ground and pointing the other up through the opening in the roof. Pushing and pulling, the men took the women with them, and their children and animals, and climbed up the reed. And when they emerged through the hole at the top, they saw that it was not really a hole in the roof but a hole in the ground. They stood on the soil of the fourth world, the one that we call Earth.

In the Fourth World

The Earth then was not as we know it now. There was neither Sun nor Moon, and it was cold and dark, very dark. In the enveloping blackness, the people could not see and could not find wood to make fire.

'How can we make it light?' the people asked.

'I will give you light,' said Gogyeng Sowuhti, Grandmother Spider, emerging from the cave-worlds. And she began to weave a white cotton cloth, as fine and intricate as a web. 'There!' she said when the work was finished. The white cloth glowed and shimmered. But it was not enough to light the world.

'Where will we find more light? the people asked.

'Ooh, aah! Find me a seat! I'm exhausted – I can't take another step. I've been carrying this thing all the way up that reed ladder …' It was Coyote, emerging from the cave-worlds with a large jar in his arms. He had found it beneath the Earth and, being a thief by nature, he could not resist stealing it. 'Now I wonder what's inside?' By the pale light of Grandmother Spider's cloth, Coyote tentatively raised the lid of the jar. As he peered inside, the lid flew off in his face as hundreds of sparks exploded from the jar, singeing his muzzle as they went (which is why it is black to this day). The sparks shot up into the sky where they became the stars that twinkle in the night.

Now there was a little more light but it was still not enough. So the chiefs and the people got together to decide what they should do. After much discussion and argument, they took a buffalo hide and made it into a round shield. They painted it white and added black patterns all around the edge. When it was dry, they placed the

Kivas and the Kachina Cult

The *kivas*, in which the women so immoderately danced in the Hopi myth 'Climbing the Ladder of the Worlds' were semi-subterranean ceremonial chambers, which were accessed by means of a ladder through an entrance in the roof. Traditionally the kivas formed not only the physical but also the symbolical centre of each pueblo. This Spanish word, meaning 'people', is used to denote both a particular type of village of multi-storeyed adobe (sun-dried brick) dwellings, as well as the Indians who lived there. The Hopi belong to the group known as Desert Pueblos, the other group being the River Pueblos.

In Pueblo Indian life, the kivas were the focal point of religious ritual; it was here that sacred objects were laid out in preparation for the rituals, the most complex of which centred on the *kachina* cult. The kachinas were supernatural beings who were particularly important to the Hopi and Zuni Indians, and were believed to have been sent by the gods to teach the kachina ceremonies to the priests. According to the Hopi, the presence of these spirits was evident in mists and rainclouds, and they remained with the people for seven months of every year until July when, after 16 days of rituals, they returned home to the mountains.

Held from late winter until the end of July, these rituals were led by the priests who, dressed as kachinas – complete with kilts and elaborate masks – danced through the pueblos, connecting with the spirits and 'raising the power' to call down the rain and to bring communal happiness and wellbeing.

In a similar spirit to that of the European Santa Claus, the kachina dancers might also visit the homes of children and punish those who had misbehaved. Wooden kachina dolls, carved to represent the spirits, were also used in the religious instruction of children.

shield in a large cloth. They chose one of their young men to stand on top of the shield. Then, singing a magic song, they began to swing the cloth, backwards and forwards, backwards and forwards in ever-widening arcs until at last they let go and – *whoosh!* – threw shield and man up into the eastern sky. The man with the white shield became the Moon.

And what did the people see, in the Moon's silver light? An island of mud, surrounded by water. Was this what they had climbed through three worlds to reach? Was this to be the homeland they hoped for? No, it was not. So they called to Vulture to help them, and Vulture came and spread his great black wings over the island and fanned back the waters and blew the mud dry and pushed it into ridges and hollows that became the mountains and valleys and plains of the world. Then Elder Brother and Younger Brother came and cut channels through the mountains so that water could run through them, and so made the rivers and canyons.

Now the world was dry and wide, and there was the Moon's light to see by. But it was still cold. So again the chiefs and the people got together to decide what they should do. This time, they took a blanket they had woven while still in the cave-worlds and made it into a round shield. They painted it copper and gave it eyes and a mouth, and decorated it with patterns in other colours and with corn husks and eagle feathers and red feathers. On the forehead of the shield-face, they placed an abalone shell. Now their creation was complete.

So they laid it in a cloth as before, and chose one of their young men to stand on it. Then, singing a magic song, they began to swing the cloth, backwards and forwards, backwards and forwards in ever-widening arcs until at last they let go and – *whoosh!* – threw the shield and the man up into the eastern sky. They disappeared behind the edge of the world.

The people watched and waited. Slowly the eastern sky began to lighten and change colour – yellow, pink, orange, red – until at last, like a floating ball of fire, the man with the copper shield rose above the horizon. He had become the Sun.

It was time for the people to move on, to take up the trail to the places where they were meant to settle, where Elder Brother and Younger Brother wished them to live.

The hole in the Earth where they emerged is called the Grand Canyon. The places where they settled are the three mesas of the Colorado Plateau. The people are the *Hopitu-shinumu*, the Peaceful Ones. They are the Hopi Indians.

HOW ANIMALS MADE THE WORLD

IROQUOIS • NORTHEAST
YUCHI • SOUTHEAST
BLACKFEET • PLAINS

WATER, WATER EVERYWHERE. That's how it was in the beginning, say the Iroquois and Huron Indians. There was nothing but a wide, wide sea that stretched as far as the far horizons in every direction.

In this watery world lived a number of creatures. There was the muskrat, with its webbed feet and flat tail, and its cousin the thick-furred beaver who builds log lodges in which to live and house its young. There was the otter who slides through the water like a snake. There were salmon and other fish, too, and birds that love water – ducks with glossy plumage and gaggles of cackling geese.

But there were no people. This is the story of how they, and the Earth, came to be.

Up in the sky-country, the Great Mother Aataensic conceived in her womb the first man and the first woman. Time passed, and soon, she knew, the moment would come when she should be delivered of her children. But one day, as she was walking about, she tripped and stumbled and fell through the hole in the sky, and came tumbling, tumbling, spiralling and turning like a leaf dancing on the breeze, all the way down through the blue air towards the wide water below.

As the animals looked up they saw her coming closer and closer towards them, and went scurrying hither and thither to find a piece of earth that they could place under her to break her fall, for they did not want her to drown. The otter searched. The beaver searched. The ducks, the geese, the salmon and all the other creatures searched. But in the end it was the muskrat who found a clump of earth – not much bigger than a fist – and quickly placed it on the back of the turtle who was swimming in the water. Only just in time, too, for at that very moment, the Great Mother landed

– *thump* – on the little piece of earth that had been placed for her on the turtle's back. It was just enough to cushion her fall for her landing was as soft as if she had been dropped into a featherbed. It was here that she was delivered of the first man and the first woman and it is their children and their children's children who are all the people of the world.

As for the clump of earth that was no bigger than a fist, a very strange thing began to happen to it. The clump began to swell and grow and to spread out over the wide, wide water until it became an island and then a vast land that stretched north, south, east and west, with hills and valleys and forests and rivers. It became the Earth on which we walk, and because it still rests on the turtle's shell, the people call it Turtle Island.

And so it is, when the sea is churned into a great swell of waves, that the people say the turtle is stirring.

And so it is, when the Earth is shaken by tremours and rumblings and quakes, that the people say the turtle is stretching its limbs.

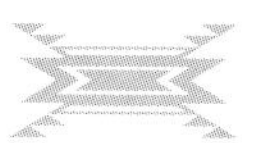

Water, water everywhere – that's how it was in the beginning, say the Yuchi Indians. There was no land; there were no people.

The Wind blew over the face of the water. He looked down into it. It was still and dark and deep. Nowhere could he see so much as a speck of soil, an outcrop of rock.

'Who will make the land appear?' Wind asked.

'I will,' said Crawfish. And he swam down to the bottom of the water. He gathered mud with his claws and piled it up in a mound. He kept adding mud to his pile until the mound he had made showed above the surface of the water.

Now there was land but it was still soft and slack, and no good for plants or animals or people.

'Who will dry out the land?' Wind asked.

'We will,' said Buzzard and

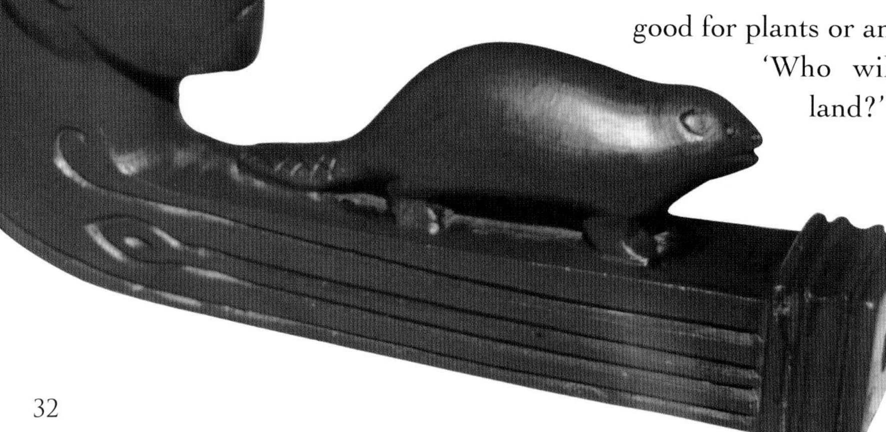

Hawk. And they flew over the mound of mud flapping their wings, blowing it dry and spreading it wide and fanning it into mountains and valleys and plains.

Now the land was firm and broad, but still it lay in darkness.

'Who will light the world?' Wind asked.

'I will,' said the Star. And, taking a deep breath and gathering up all his strength, he shone as brightly as he could. But his was only a little light, not enough to see by.

'Who will light the world?' Wind asked again.

'I will,' said the Moon. And she turned to show all of her round silver face and cast her shining gaze over the world. In her cool light, the world lay blue and shadowy and dreaming. But still there was not enough light to see by.

'Who will light the world?' Wind asked for a third time.

'I will,' said Sun. And he went to the east and crouched down behind the edge of the world and prepared himself. And then he leapt into the sky, and so blindingly bright was his face that it lit up all of creation and chased away the shadows.

But the effort of his first rising caused the Sun to bleed a little and, as he travelled across the sky to his home in the west, he let a few drops of blood fall down onto the land below. In the place where they fell, strange new beings arose, like little shoots out of the soil. These new beings were the first people. They were the Yuchi Indians, born of the blood of the Sun.

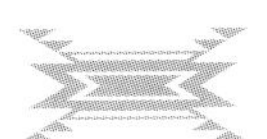

Water, water everywhere. That's how it was in the beginning, say the Blackfeet Indians.

Old Man Napi sat floating on a log, gazing at the water and wondering. Next to him sat Otter, Duck, Beaver and Muskrat.

'What lies below the water?' Napi thought. So he sent Otter to find out.

With a flip of his sleek body, Otter dived out of sight. But he never returned. Perhaps he was enjoying his swim too much.

So Napi sent Duck. Upending herself so that only her fat tail and webbed feet stuck out of the water, she disappeared. She never came back. Perhaps she is still underwater, feasting on insects and snails and small fish.

So Napi sent Beaver. Beaver was good at digging, so he dived deep into the water and began to rootle around at the bottom. He never returned. Perhaps he has dug himself a new burrow, down at the bottom of the sea.

So Napi sent Muskrat. Muskrat loved the water. He paddled off onto it, steering with his flattened tail. And then he disappeared beneath the surface.

Five minutes went by. Ten. Twenty. Then the water began to bubble and froth, and Muskrat leapt out. In his feet, he carried a lump of mud.

Sitting on his log, Napi took the mud and began rolling it between his hands, and as he rolled it the lump grew bigger. He dropped it back into the water and it spread out in all directions and became the land on which we walk. And that, say the Blackfeet Indians, is how Napi and Muskrat made the world, so long, long ago.

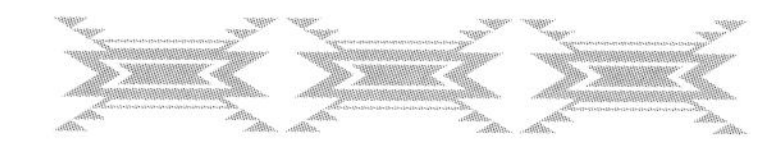

The Buffalo Skin Sky

PLATEAU AND BASIN

In the beginning, people lived at peace with the Earth and all her creatures. The Great Spirit had said that it should be so.

'The Earth is your mother and the animals are your brothers,' he told them, 'and you must protect them. Above all, take care of the buffalo. He gives you his flesh for food and his hide for clothing. As long as you have the buffalo, you will be safe and well.'

In the north, the south, the east and the west, the people heard what the Great Spirit said. In the Yellowstone Valley, they heard it, too, and they obeyed. When they killed a buffalo, they gave thanks to it for its life. They used every part of the beast so that nothing was wasted. When they hunted the deer or the moose, or caught the trout, the grayling or the whitefish, or saw the swan on the lake, the cougar in the mountains or the eagle in the sky, they called each by its name: 'Brother,' they said. And so they lived their lives in this way for many generations, taking only what they needed and being grateful for what they had.

But then new people came. They ignored the words of the Great Spirit. They believed that the Earth and the animals were theirs for the taking. They took what they wanted and what they took they wasted. They burned and destroyed the forests where the animals lived. They hunted the buffalo for sport, not for food. Soon there were hardly any buffalo left.

Up in the sky-country, the Great Spirit was watching. He saw the smoke of the forest fires, and he was angry. He stopped the smoke from rising so that it hung in drifts near the ground, making the people choke and cough.

And still they ignored him. Still they continued in their destructive ways.

So the Great Spirit sent a rain to put out the fires and drown the people. It rained and it rained and it rained, and the people were swept away in the rising tide – all, that is, except for a few who remembered the Great Spirit's words.

'Come,' said their leader, a medicine man. 'Let us go and find the buffalo. As long as we have them, the Great Spirit said, we will be safe and well.'

So they climbed up into the hills, away from the flooded plains. And still it rained and the waters rose.

So the people climbed higher, up into the mountains. And still it rained and the waters rose.

So they climbed up to the mountaintops, and set up camp there.

Meanwhile, the young men among them had been out hunting, to look for buffalo. Two of them returned. 'We have seen them – we have seen the buffalo!' they said. 'A white bull, a cow and a calf. We killed the bull and took his hide, but his body was washed away by the flood. The cow and the calf escaped, and we did too, just as the water reached our ankles. Here – here is the bull's hide ...' And they laid before their people the skin of a huge white buffalo bull.

The chief medicine man and the other holy men took the skin and scraped it and stretched it. And as the rain continued to fall and wetted the buffalo hide it became even more elastic. The medicine men stretched it over the camp, and the people huddled under its protective cover as if under a giant umbrella.

Still it rained.

The medicine men continued to stretch the white buffalo skin, taking its corners and hooking them onto the peaks of the mountains so that it covered the whole of Yellowstone Valley.

Still the rain fell. But in the Valley, beneath the buffalo skin, it was dry.

The people returned to the Valley and began their lives again. The animals returned, too, and the people welcomed them and called each by its name: 'Brother,' they said.

Still the rain fell. It collected in puddles and pools on top of the white buffalo skin and made it sag. So the chief medicine man went to the top of a mountain to the east of the Valley and lifted one corner of the skin, just enough to let in the West Wind.

'Come, Wind, come,' he called. And the West Wind flew in under the skin and huffed and puffed and blew, filling the space with air and pushing up the sagging skin so that it ballooned into a mighty dome over the Valley.

Up in the sky-country, the Great Spirit had been watching. He saw the people return. He saw that they once again lived at peace with the Earth and all her creatures.

He stopped the rain.

He parted the clouds.

He let the Sun shine through.

As the warm Sun shone down on the white buffalo skin, the skin began to glow, reflecting the Sun's prismatic light. In the heat, it began to shrink, too, pulling away from its moorings on the mountaintops and slowly diminishing in size from a dome to a half-sphere to an arch. The arch spanned the Valley from one side to the other, and shimmered with iridescent colour. Red, orange, yellow, green, blue, violet and indigo. It was a rainbow. And there beneath it, grazing on the new, waving, flower-strewn grass, were the white buffalo cow and her calf.

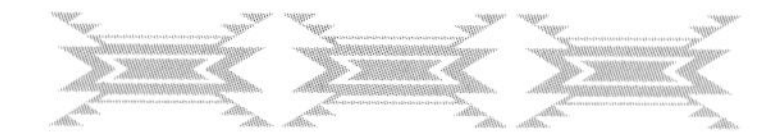

THE TWO-MEN-WHO-CHANGED-THINGS

MAKAH • NORTHWEST COAST

IN THE BEGINNING WHEN THE WORLD WAS NEW, there were no people, only a rag-taggle company of curious creatures: Things who were neither bird nor beast, neither fish nor fowl, neither this nor that, neither one nor the other, but had, in their indefinable natures, a little something of everything. In the newly born world, the Things roamed aimlessly, doing as they pleased. Some fished, some hunted, some thieved.

The two brothers of the Sun and Moon saw what was happening. 'This cannot go on,' they said. So they came to Earth to give the nameless Things their names and bring order to the world, to make it ready for the coming of humankind. They were *Ho-ho-e-ap-bess*, the Two-Men-Who-Changed-Things.

'Hey, you – thief!' they shouted at a creature who was just making off with the fishing catch of another. 'Your thieving days are over. From

THE POTLATCH

When the Two-Men-Who-Changed-Things created the animals and plants, they apportioned to each an identity and a place in the world. In a similar way, the humans who came after them also 'knew their place'. The social organization of the tribes of the Northwest Coast region was highly hierarchical, consisting of three classes who might be called nobles, commoners and slaves. The way to demonstrate and maintain social position was through wealth, and the vehicle devised to do this was the *potlatch*.

Derived from a Chinook term meaning 'to give', the potlatch took the form of a feast held to celebrate a special event – a birth, wedding, or death perhaps, or the acquisition of a social title or the raising of a totem pole – and was accompanied by the formal giving of gifts. It had a more profound function, too, for it reinforced social relationships and hierarchies, encouraged the economic system of exchange and barter, and preserved cultural heritage.

Potlatches were held in the winter and lasted several days. Preparations began well ahead, with the host accumulating a supply of food and material goods to offer as gifts for the guests. In order to acquire sufficient goods, he – or sometimes she – would loan possessions to others and would then be 'paid back' with items to the same value and more.

The guests at the potlatch came from other kinship groups and villages, and received gifts according to their rank. By accepting them, they publicly acknowledged and validated the donor's status, for example, his or her right to a hereditary title. The guests, in their turn, would have to reciprocate with potlatches of their own, at which they had at least to match, if not exceed, the gifts of their former host if they wished to maintain their social standing. The potlatch was therefore a highly competitive custom, and one which the Kwakiutl of British Columbia perceptively referred to as 'fighting with property'. Such was the pressure to excel in gift-giving that the host and his or her family often found themselves bereft of possessions afterwards, a state of affairs which horrified European observers and led to the banning of the custom by the Canadian government between 1854 and 1951. The Indians continued to practise it, however.

As well as feasting and gift-giving, the potlatch also involved long speeches and traditional songs, dances and dramatic performances using headdresses, masks and other items of ceremonial clothing, which recalled family and tribal history and taught the watching children.

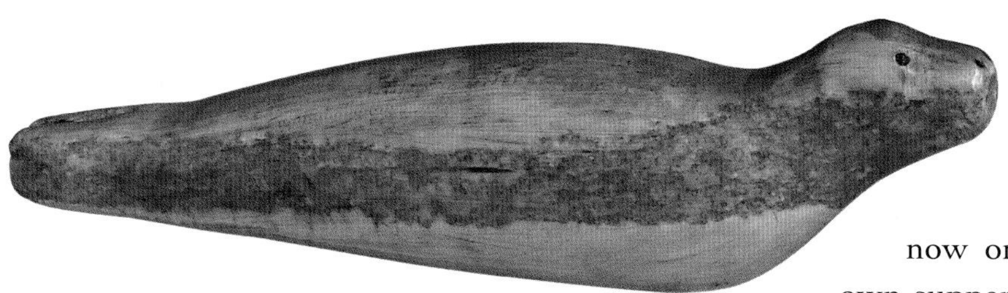

now on, you will fish for your own supper.' And as they spoke, the creature began to change. Its arms shrank and became flippers. Its legs fused and became a tail. Only its feet at the end flapped free. The Two-Men pushed the creature into the sea.

'You are Seal,' they said.

In the shallows of a stream stood a tall, thin creature, with a white cape around its slender shoulders. Its skinny legs were planted knee-deep in the water. Not a limb moved, not a muscle flickered as it pierced the water with its beady gaze. Whenever a fish came swimming by, it impaled it with the spear it carried.

As the brothers focused their eyes on it, it began to change. Its cape became a ring of white feathers. Its spear became a beak.

'You are Heron,' the Two-Men said.

On a branch overlooking the stream perched another creature – a small, bright-eyed Thing with a blue cape and a ring of shells around its neck. It, too, was watching for fish. Having no spear like Heron, it was obliged to dive underwater for its catch. As the brothers looked at it, the ring of shells it wore became a ring of feathers.

'You are Kingfisher,' the Two-Men said.

In a clearing in the forest, two creatures were arguing over some scraps of meat – black angry Things with coarse, rasping voices. 'That is mine!' cried one. 'No, it's mine!' yelled the other, snatching the titbit from the mouth of its mate, for the pair were husband and wife. They neither hunted nor fished but scavenged, daily gorging themselves on whatever food they could find.

'You are Raven,' said the Two-Men to the husband, and, 'You are Crow,' to the wife.

'Caw, caw,' Crow and Raven replied, and returned to their feast, tearing it up with their sharp beaks.

The next creature that the brothers encountered belonged to both land and water, living on one and catching its food in the other.

'Which would you be?' they asked it. 'A bird? Or a fish?'

'Neither,' the creature replied.

'Then you are Mink,' the Two-Men said. And Mink it has been ever since, enjoying the best of both worlds.

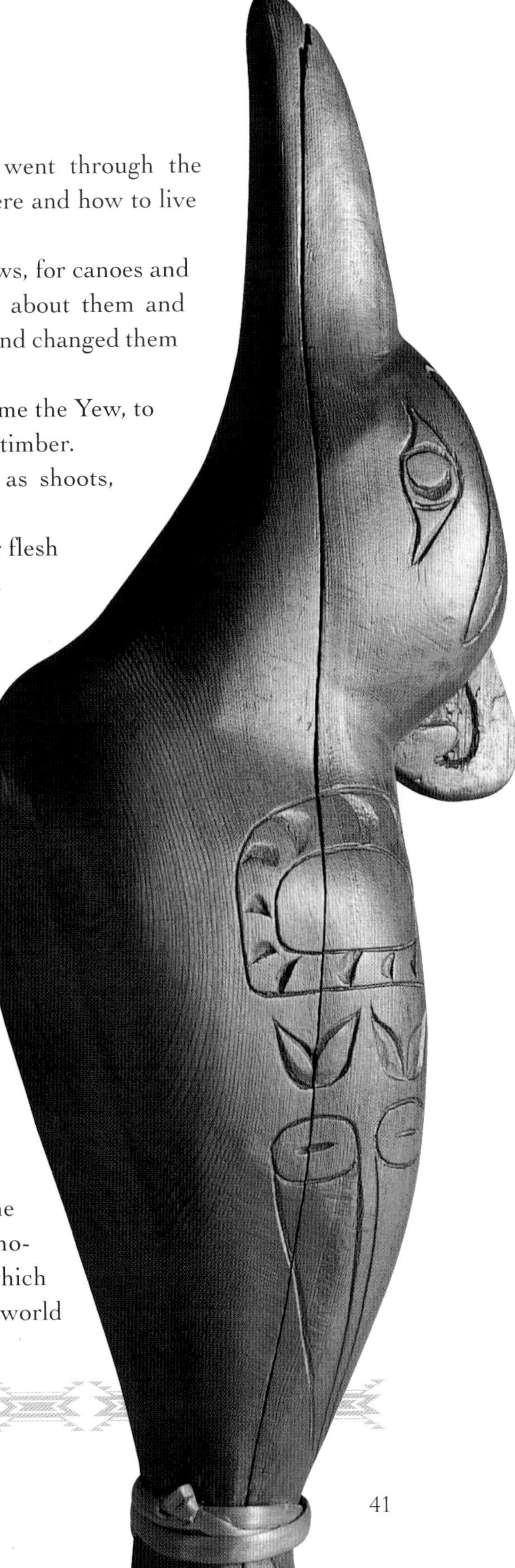

And so the Two-Men-Who-Changed-Things went through the world, naming the creatures and telling them where and how to live and what to eat. But their work was not yet done.

'Humans will need wood for bows and for arrows, for canoes and for fuel,' the two brothers said. So they looked about them and chose those creatures best fitted to each purpose, and changed them into trees.

One that was especially tough and strong became the Yew, to provide wood for bows and wedges for splitting timber.

A gaggle of little ones, slender and straight as shoots, became the wood that was used for arrows.

One with a wide girth and soft, sweet-smelling flesh became the Cedar, used in the making of canoes.

One with a tall, hardened body became the Alder, to provide wood for canoe paddles.

Another, aged and stick-dry, became the Spruce, used when old as firewood.

One whose skin, when pierced, oozed a thick, reddish liquid became the Hemlock, whose bark provided tannin for treating hides, and whose branches were used in the sweat-lodge fires to give off purifying smoke.

Another, short of temper and sour of face, became the Crab Apple tree, whose fruit was as acid as its temperament.

And one with a sweet temper and a generous nature became the Wild Cherry, who willingly gave people its fruit for food and its bark for medicine.

When all the naming and the sorting and the apportioning was done, the Two-Men-Who-Changed-Things returned to the place from which they had come. What they left behind was a world made ready for the human race.

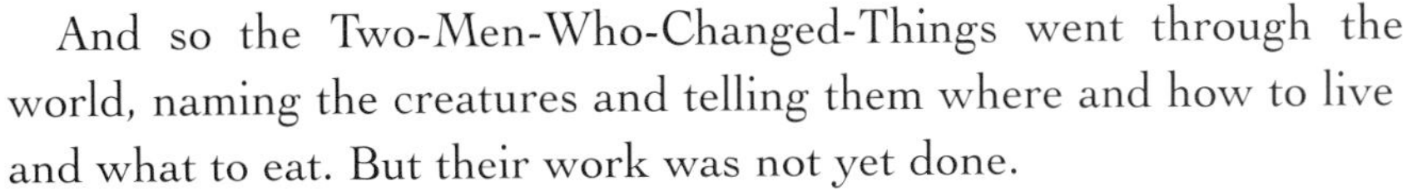

TRICKSTERS AND CULTURE HEROES

HOW SPIDERMAN WAS TRICKED BY HIS WIFE

SIOUX • PLAINS

SPIDERMAN IKTOMI LOVED WOMEN. Whether waking or sleeping, he thought about them – big women, small women, laughing women, shy women, voluptuous maidens and blossoming girls paraded for his pleasure across the field of his imagination, and he was always on the lookout for his next conquest.

'They cannot resist me,' he told himself smugly, stroking his skinny little body and admiring his spidery little legs. 'What a great lover I am – how skilled, how potent, how vigorous!'

And it is true that Iktomi was not without his triumphs, for what he lacked in looks he more than made up for in trickery and guile. He could turn himself into a handsome young warrior in less time than it takes to turn a hair. He possessed a love medicine that blinded women to all other men. He could play the flute so magically that it drew women to him like bees to honey. And – best of all – his manhood was so large that he carried it about in a box, and could extend it to an even greater length to reach the object of his desire, or detach it and send it off to do its pleasurable work. Oh, how fortunate he was to be thus endowed!

There was one small complication, however. Iktomi already had a wife, who was wise to his infidelities and his tricks. But even that did not stop him – he could not and would not stop chasing other women.

One day, he noticed an especially beautiful young woman in the village. Why, he asked himself, had he not spotted her before? Her skin was smooth and golden, her hair sleek and raven-black, her lips flushed pink, her breasts full, her eyes like pools of water peeping out from beneath thickly fringed lashes. *Mmm, mmm*! Now here was a ripe fruit, ready for picking!

Iktomi sat and slyly and hungrily watched the young woman as she came with the

others to collect water from the stream.

He picked up his flute and began to woo her with music. But the young woman seemed immune to his charms. Incredible! He would have to try another tactic.

He sidled up to her. 'You know ...' he oozed, 'I could make you very happy. Let me show you how ...'

'Oh no, you don't!' said the young woman, pushing him away, for she knew Iktomi's reputation and was not fooled by his flattering tongue.

'Well,' thought Iktomi, 'a little resistance only adds to the fun – after all, the fruit that falls straight into your hand is a fruit not worth having.' So he followed the young woman about, trilling love songs on his pipe and cooing suggestive sweet nothings to her whenever he could get close enough. But despite all his skill and experience in such matters, she remained unmoved.

After several days of his persistent and unwanted attentions, her irritation at him bubbled over. She went to see his wife.

'Has my husband been trying to seduce you?' said the wife to the girl.

'Your husband has been trying to seduce me,' said the girl to the wife.

'Let us teach him a lesson,' said the wife.

'How?' said the girl.

'We will exchange places – I will pretend to be you.'

'What will you give me for helping you?'

'I will give you my necklace of beads.'

'And what else?'

'My quilled buckskin dress.'

'It is done.'

And so the bargain was struck. The wife and the girl exchanged clothes. The girl went to the wife's tipi and the wife, with head demurely lowered so that he would not recognize her face, went to find her husband.

'You know,' she began, fluttering her eyelashes and speaking in a soft, girlish voice. 'Perhaps I have been too hard on you. I hear you are a great lover ...'

Iktomi puffed out his chest with pride: 'I am, indeed yes, I am.'

'And maybe I would be foolish to miss such an experience ...'

'Oh you would, yes indeed, you would.'

'Then come to my tipi tonight. Only my grandmother lives with me and she is deaf and will not hear us.'

Iktomi was almost beside himself with excitement and lust. He could not wait for the

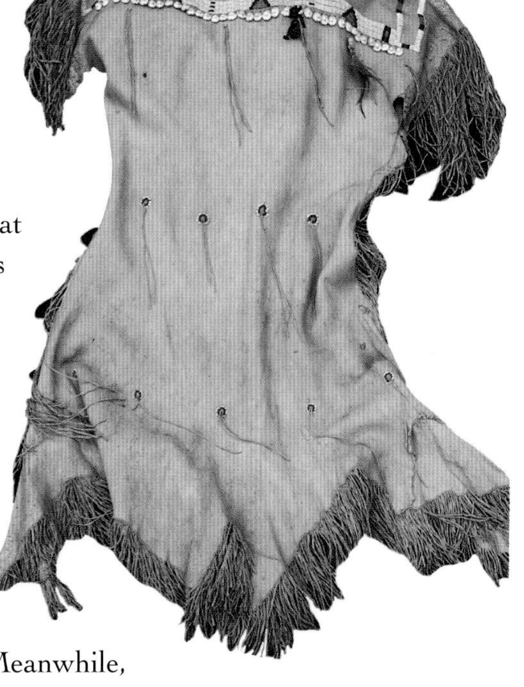

Sun to go down. At last, as the soft mantle of night descended, he crept into the girl's tipi. Her grandmother lay on one side, snoring and dead to the world. *She* lay on the other, breathless and waiting. Iktomi slid in beside her.

'Oh, my beauty, how long I have waited for this moment!' he panted.

He began to kiss her. 'Oh what tender lips, what sweet breath ... not like the reek from my wife's mouth ...'

He began to caress her. 'Oh what soft curves, what firm breasts ... not like the sagging dugs of my wife, her puckered flesh ...'

He slipped between her legs. 'Oh how receptive you are, how moist ... not like my wife who lies there like a dried-up lump of wood ...'

When he had done what he came to do, he rose from the bed and began – slowly, for his exertions had left him exhausted – to make his way home. Meanwhile, his wife ran ahead of him and changed places with the girl so that when he finally arrived at their tipi, all was as it should be, with his wife fast asleep in her place and apparently none the wiser.

'Aaah ...' Iktomi sank down beside her with a long, satisfied sigh. He had got away with it again.

When he woke the following morning, the Sun was already high in the sky. His wife was up and busying herself with her chores. Iktomi yawned and stretched.

'How hungry I am. Give me something to eat,' he said, 'something nice.'

'I'll give you something all right!' replied his wife, picking up a stick. 'How about "reeking breath"?' She brought the stick down on his back. 'Or would you like some "sagging dugs"? Or some "puckered flesh"?' *Bash!* The stick slammed down again. 'Or perhaps you'd prefer a "dried-up lump of wood"?' *Bang, smash!* The stick whizzed past his ear and cracked against the side of his skull.

When his wife had finally finished with him, Spiderman Iktomi was black and blue all over. He stayed inside their tipi for at least a week, nursing his wounds and pondering over the injustice of it all.

But even this beating did not teach him a lesson, and it wasn't long before the great lover was out flirting and philandering again, for he could not give up his old ways.

HOW COYOTE STOLE FIRE

NORTHWEST COAST

COYOTE STOOD ON A MOUNTAINTOP, looking out over the land. He saw the Sun sinking behind the western hills. He saw blue-black forests of spruce and cedar that wrapped the slopes like a blanket. He saw a river that flowed like a silver ribbon through gullies and canyons; and in the far, far distance he saw something he had never seen before – a tiny light flickering in the growing darkness like the tongue of a snake.

He decided to investigate. If this snake-tongue of light was any good, he would steal it for himself. But he might need some help. So he called the animals – Deer, Bear, Wolf, Fox and other beasts – to him.

'Come on,' he said, 'we're going on a journey.'

The animals agreed to go with him and the party set off.

At last they reached their destination. It was a large lodge. In the middle, feeding on a pile of crackling logs, was the snake-tongue light, darting and flashing and quivering. The light that Coyote had seen was fire, and this was the home of the Fire People, who guarded the flame.

'Oh, how tired we are,' said Coyote to the Fire People. 'We could not have gone on another step – we have found you only just in time.' And he made a great show of puffing and mopping his brow, as if to prove his exhaustion.

Like all good hosts, the Fire People made their guests welcome and prepared for a dance in their honour. Coyote made himself a special costume for the occasion – a headdress of pine shavings and bark fringes which reached all the way to the ground.

The Fire People began the dance, proceeding in a swaying circle around the flames. Then it was Coyote's turn.

'No, no,' he said, 'it's much too dark to dance. I can't see a thing. I might trip over my own feet and break a leg!'

The Fire People added more logs to the fire to increase the light from the blaze.

'Impossible! It's still as black as the inside of a cave. How can you live in such darkness?

The People stoked up the fire to such a pitch that the flames stretched their flickering fingers high above their heads. The heat was almost intolerable.

'Oh, how scorching it is,' cried Coyote's

Tricksters and Totem Animals

Anarchic, amoral, irreverent and opportunistic, the trouble-making Trickster makes his appearance in almost every mythology around the world. He is the cunning prankster who defies divine authority and the natural order of things. He is the fire-bringer and ally of mankind. He is a supernatural shape-shifter and, often, a creator; rarely, he is a malevolent force. For the Greeks, he was Prometheus who defied Zeus to steal fire from heaven. For the Norse people, he was the devious Loki; for the Polynesians, he was Maui who tried to cheat Death and who fished New Zealand out of the ocean. In Africa, he was Spiderman Anansi; in the Deep South, he was Brer Rabbit (who passed his genes to Bugs Bunny).

Similarly, to the first people of North America, he revealed himself in animal form, appearing as Spider, Rabbit, the Great Hare Nanabozho, Blue Jay, Raven and – above all – Coyote. These animal manifestations of the Trickster varied according to region. Thus, for example, Spiderman Iktomi was revered by the Sioux of the Plains and Raven was the arch Trickster of the Pacific Northwest. Coyote, however, was active across the whole continent from north to south.

The Trickster animal-man was a larger-than-life figure, but particular species were venerated on a much more local level, too, when they were known as 'totems', a name derived from the Algonquian word *ototeman*. A totem animal was one with whom an individual or group was believed to have a mystical bond. Often, the animal was seen as the progenitor of a clan, and its protector, with supernatural powers which earned it both respect and fear. Through this shared animal ancestor, the clan was related to animals of the same species, and was therefore prohibited from killing and eating them except in ritual sacrifice. (With the same logic, they often practised exogamy – marriage outside of the clan – for to marry within it would have been incestuous.)

The so-called 'totem poles' carved from red cedar by the Indians of the Northwest Coast do not, in fact, show totem animals, but served as heraldic crests which provided a visual record of a family's lineage. They might be placed outside the homes of their owners, or used to mark graves.

animal allies, fanning themselves ostentatiously as they joined in his game. 'We shall have to go outside to cool ourselves.'

But Coyote stayed inside and began to dance. He circled the bonfire, whirling and swirling and prancing faster and faster and swishing the tails and fringes of his headdress closer and closer to the flames until what he wanted to happen did happen.

His headdress caught fire.

He ran out of the lodge, an arrow of flame, with the Fire People close behind him.

Coyote threw the burning headdress to Deer, who threw it to Bear, who threw it to Wolf, who threw it to Fox, and so on through all the other beasts. As the headdress passed down the line, the Fire People caught each animal in turn and killed him. In the end only Coyote was left.

Coyote stood alone, holding the sacred gift of fire. But he had no one to give it to, so he passed it to the nearest tree.

Trees have guarded fire ever since. That is why, when people want to have fire, they kindle it from the wood of trees.

How Raven Brought the Daylight

TLINGIT/TSIMSHIAN • NORTHWEST COAST

RAVEN IS A LIAR and Raven is a thief and Raven is a lazy, greedy, good-for-nothing cheat. Raven was here before the beginning. He has many names. He is *Yehl*. He is *Txamsem*. He is *Kwekwaxa'we*. He is *Nankil'slas*. He is the maker of the world.

Raven put his giant cloak of feathers on his giant body and went to survey the world. It was dark, too dark. But he knew just where to find light. In the Sky Country.

He flew up and squeezed himself through the hole in the sky. There was the house of the Sky Chief. Raven watched and saw the chief's daughter coming to collect water from the spring. *Mmm, mmm,* she was beautiful. He would enjoy this task!

He changed himself into a tiny speck of life – the merest germ, invisible to the eye – and plopped into the water she was carrying. The girl did not notice. She raised the water to her lips, and swallowed. Nine months later, she gave birth to a baby boy.

'Caw!' the baby screamed. 'Caw-w-w-w!'

'Why is my little precious crying?' said his grandfather. 'Does he want – this?' And he held out a wooden spoon.

MEDICINE MEN

In his aspect as creator and benefactor who can 'grow' the whole world from a lump of mud or bring the miracle of fire to humankind, the Trickster is not so much a god as a kind of super-shaman, a wonder-working magician who straddles the human and supernatural worlds. In Native American tradition, the Trickster takes animal form, and many shamans were similarly believed to have the power to 'shape-shift' into animal guise.

Another name for the North American shaman is 'medicine man' (or woman, for the role could be taken by a female), 'medicine' being both supernatural potency as well as healing power. The medicine man was the magician-priest who acted as an intermediary between the community and the spirit world, and was thus able to effect cures, foretell the future, and generally act for the benefit of the individual or group. He – or she – could literally, it was believed, travel into the realm of the unseen and communicate directly with the spirits. He also had his own spirit helper or helpers – which, like the familiars of the European witch, were often spirit animals – as well as a collection of magical objects which he could use to call on these helpers.

As well as herbal remedies, the medicine man used supernatural cures to treat those illnesses thought to have a supernatural cause. He might, for example, send his own soul to bring back the exiled soul of the afflicted individual, carrying a 'soul-catcher', consisting of a carved bone or wooden tube, to help him. This shamanic journey would be undertaken while in a state of ecstatic trance, perhaps induced by narcotics or frantic dancing. If the medicine man lived in the Pacific Northwest, he would enact a canoe voyage to the world of the dead, in order to invite his spirit helpers to make the actual journey to retrieve the patient's soul. Alternatively, a shaman might suck the disease from the patient's body.

As well as being a healer, the shaman was a seer. One technique used was 'reading the bones', or scapulimancy, as practised in the Sub-Arctic region, for example. In this procedure, the shaman would hold the shoulder-blade bones of caribou, moose or hare over the fire until they blackened and cracked, and would then interpret the future from the patterns.

The magical powers possessed by the shaman or medicine man made him a figure both to respect and to fear, and thus set him apart from the community he served. When he died his body and all the tools of his trade were often buried away from the village because, even in death, they were still highly charged with the supernatural and were therefore dangerous.

'Caw!' bawled the baby.

'Or this?' He held out a bone comb.

'Caw-*caw!*' howled the baby.

'Or this?' And he held out a carved wooden box, the first of three.

The baby stopped crying and grabbed the box in his plump, dimpled little hands. He examined it, turning it over and over. He pushed it around the floor. He picked it up and threw it – *smash!* The lid blew off and all the stars exploded out. They flew through the smoke-hole in the roof and went to their places in the sky.

'*Caw-aw-aw-w-w!*' screeched the baby.

'No, no, no, my duckling, my little owlet, don't cry – here, have this!' And his grandfather held out another wooden box, richly carved, the second of three.

The baby snatched it and went silent. He turned the box this way and that, upside-down, on its side, but he could not open it. He screwed up his face in frustrated rage and threw the box across the room. The lid blew off and out rose the Moon. It flew out through the smoke-hole in the roof and took its place in the sky.

'CAW!' shrieked the baby. His eardrum-shattering howl shook the universe. Why would he not stop crying? Was he cold? Was he hungry? Was he lonely? Was he bored? What could it be? His grandfather could not stand it a moment longer.

'Here!' he shouted, and pushed at his grandson the last of the three wooden boxes, the one that was the most beautiful of all.

The baby seized the box and stood up. He changed into Raven – for he had been Raven all along – and flew out through the smoke-hole in the roof.

'Stop, thief!' all the Sky People cried. But it was too late. Raven was already squeezing through the hole in heaven. And then he was gone.

Raven raised the lid of the box he was carrying. With a blinding white flash, it blew off and out burst the Sun, to take its place in the sky.

'*Caw-w-w* ...' he sighed.

And that is how Raven brought light to the world. It is said that before that day – the day he let the Sun out of the box – he was as white as a swan. But as he flew through the smoke-hole of the house of the chief of heaven, the soot dirtied his feathers. He has been as black as night ever since.

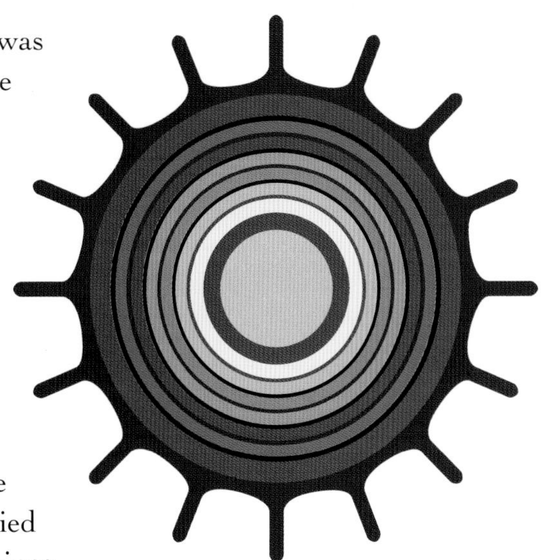

HOW RABBIT CAUGHT THE SUN

OMAHA • PLAINS

RABBIT WAS A CREATURE OF HABIT. Every morning he picked up his bow and arrows, left the tipi he shared with his grandmother, and set off to hunt. And every morning someone followed him. A tall, thin, dark, silent shape.

'Who are you?' asked Rabbit.

But the shape said nothing. It just kept following Rabbit wherever he went, sticking to his heels like glue.

When Rabbit ran, it ran.

When Rabbit stopped, it stopped.

When Rabbit crouched and took aim with his bow, the shape did too.

'Get away from me! Leave me alone!' Rabbit cried. He was getting scared, and worse – he was beginning to lose his concentration. How could a hunter be expected to do his job with someone standing behind him, copying his every move, mocking him and making fun of him?

Rabbit began getting up earlier and earlier, hoping to escape his pursuer. But it was no good. As soon as he set foot outside the tipi and into the light of morning, there as always was his tall, thin, dark, silent companion, lurking … waiting for him.

'*Aaah!*' yelled Rabbit, breaking into a run. The shape broke into a run too, and came slithering and sliding, flitting and floating, lolloping and leaping after him, over dirt, over stones, through grass and scrub. Rabbit could not shake it off.

'What is happening to me?' he thought, mopping the sweat of fear off his brow and trying to stop his hands from trembling. 'Am I being haunted? Is this a ghost?' The only peace he had was at night, for the shape seemed to disappear as soon as darkness fell.

'What is happening to you?' his grandmother asked him that evening as he sat eating, nervously darting glances over his shoulder. 'You're a shadow of your old self.'

So it went on for days – weeks – until at last Rabbit's fear turned to anger. 'I've had enough of this!' he said. So he took the string of his bow and made it into a snare. He placed the snare over the footprints he had left, just outside the tipi. Then he snuggled up under his pile of skins to enjoy a deep and dreamless sleep.

Early the following morning, just before the Sun was due to rise above the eastern ridge of the world, Rabbit left his bed and went to check his snare. He found that it had done its work. But the object caught in it was not the object he expected – it was, instead, a huge, round, shining ball, so bright that Rabbit could not look directly at it, and so hot that he could hardly go near it.

'Release me at once!' it roared, scorching the grass with its burning breath and threatening to set the prairie on fire. 'How dare you trap me like this! Don't you know who I am?'

'Who are you, then?' asked Rabbit, in awe.

'I am the Sun, of course, you idiot! Now set me free, or I will burn you and your grandmother and your tipi to a blackened crisp!'

Rabbit did not want to end his days as nothing more than a charred memory. He also wanted his bowstring back. So he ran into the tipi to fetch his knife. Lowering his eyes so they would not be blinded and steeling himself against the heat so fierce it could melt flesh, Rabbit quickly cut the string.

The Sun, set free at last, leapt up into the sky, like a stone shot from a catapult.

Rabbit flopped, exhausted, on the ground. The experience did not leave him unmarked. Ever since that day, he has had a dark smudge between his shoulder blades, a scorchmark from going too near the Sun.

As for the tall, thin, dark, silent shape that followed him – well, it is still there, but only in the mornings and evenings when the Sun is low over the horizon and casts his long light across the land. At midday, when the Sun is high overhead, Rabbit does not see his shadow at all.

NANABOZHO AND THE FLOOD

ALGONQUIAN • NORTHEAST

ONE DAY NANABOZHO WAS OUT HUNTING WITH HIS WOLF PACK. They came to a great lake. But instead of turning to run along the shore the animals, in their excitement, thundered on, plunging into the water and sinking into its silent depths.

Nanabozho waded in to try to save them. As he forced his way into the lake, the movement of his powerful limbs and the swirling of his wild breath stirred the water to a storm and sent great waves pitching and rolling out over the shore, carrying everything in their path. Rocks and boulders were borne along like little pebbles and leaves were stripped off the trees, as Nanabozho swam.

When he finally stopped, the whole world was covered with water.

Nowhere could he see one single spot of dry land. So he called Raven to him.

'Go out across the water,' he said, 'and bring back a single grain of soil. Then I can make a new world out of the old.'

With a croak and a swish of feathers, Raven flew off. But when he returned, his beak was empty. So Nanabozho called Otter.

'Go out into the water,' he said, 'and bring back a single grain of soil. Then I can make a new world out of the old.'

With a flip of his sleek body, Otter dived into the water and was soon out of sight. But when he returned, his paws were empty. So Nanabozho called Muskrat.

'Go out into the water,' he said as before, 'and bring back a single grain of soil. Then I can make a new world out of the old.'

Muskrat slipped into the water and disappeared. She was gone a long time – one hour, two hours, three ... a day ... a week, who knows? But when she returned, she held in her paws the smallest, muddiest, stickiest lump of earth.

Nanabozho took the lump of earth. He breathed on it and said secret words and set it to float on the water. And the little lump grew and grew until it had become an island and then a vast land, with hills and valleys and plains and trees. But the trees had no branches or leaves, so Nanabozho lifted his bow and shot arrows into the trunks, and these took root in the bark and became leafy branches. And this new world that he made was more beautiful than you can imagine.

Nor did he forget who had helped him. He took Muskrat as his wife, and it is you and I and all the human race who are their children's children's children, and who live in this beautiful world that Nanabozho made.

GLOOSKAP AND MALSUM

ALGONQUIAN • NORTHEAST

GLOOSKAP THE LIAR and Malsum the Wolf were twins, two fruits from the same flower. Their mother died giving them life. From her body Glooskap made the Sun and the Moon, animals, fishes and people; Malsum made mountains and valleys, snakes and all manner of troublesome creatures.

'Tell me, Brother,' said Malsum to Glooskap, 'are you truly immortal, as they say? Or is there, somewhere in the wide, wide world, one thing that can harm you?'

'Well, Brother,' replied Glooskap, 'it is a secret. No one else knows it. But I will tell it to you. Come here …' And, beckoning, he whispered in Malsum's ear, 'The one thing

in the wide, wide world that can kill me is an owl's feather.'

'Aah!' sighed Malsum. 'So that's how it is.'

'And now,' continued Glooskap, 'I have told you my secret – you must tell me yours.'

'Well, Brother, you see, it is like this: the one thing in the wide, wide world that can kill me is a blow from a fern-root.'

'Aah!' said Glooskap. 'So that's how it is.'

From that moment on, Malsum could think only of killing his brother. He went out, raised his bow, shot down an owl, and took one of its feathers. As soon as Glooskap was asleep, he stroked him with it. Glooskap moaned, groaned, and died.

But a minute later, he was sitting up again. 'Oh, what a deep sleep that was. Do you know – I had the strangest dream. I dreamed that you tried to kill me by touching me with an owl's feather. Who gave you that idea?'

'You did.'

'Dear Brother, you are quite mistaken. I never said any such thing. No – and I confide this to you because you are my own flesh and blood – the one thing in the wide, wide world that can kill me is a pine-root.'

'Aah!' said Malsum. 'So that's how it is.'

He could hardly wait. The next time Glooskap fell asleep, he crept up to him and – *tap, tap* – struck him lightly with a length of pine-root.

'Ha, ha, ha, hee, hee ... no, stop!' cried Glooskap, squirming and laughing. 'That tickles! You weren't trying to kill me again? It would take more than a bit of pine-root to do that!' And he got up and wandered off to the riverbank. He sat down by the water's edge. 'Ah, dear Brother, if only you knew ... the one thing in the wide, wide world with the power to kill me is a flowering rush.'

Down in the reeds, Beaver overheard. He went at once to Malsum.

'What will you give me if I tell you a secret – if I tell you how to kill your brother?'

'Whatever your heart desires.'

'Well,' said Beaver, preening and combing his fur with his claws, 'I have always had a fancy to fly. Before I tell you your brother's secret, you must give me wings like the wings of a bird!'

'*You!* Fly like a bird! You great ugly lump! There aren't wings big enough to get you off the ground!' And Malsum roared with mocking laughter.

Beaver was furious. He decided to get his revenge. He went to Glooskap and told him the whole story.

Glooskap was furious. The time for games was over. He dug up a fern-root. He waited until Malsum was asleep. He touched him with the root and killed him. Stock, stone, dead.

GLOOSKAP AND THE FOUR WISHES

ALGONQUIAN (MICMAC) • NORTHEAST

COILS OF MIST DRIFT OVER THE SEA LIKE GHOSTS. In the middle of the mist lies an island. On the island lives Glooskap. The mist is the smoke from his pipe.

It became known that Glooskap had the power to grant wishes. And so it was, one fine day, that four men set off to visit him, in search of their hearts' desires.

The first man, who was poor, dreamed only of being rich. 'How much happier I would be if I were free of the burden of poverty ...' he thought, 'the burden of wealth I would joyfully bear!'

The second man, who was short, dreamed only of being tall. 'I am tired of being small and puny, I am weary of being scorned,' he thought. 'If I were tall, people would admire and respect me.'

The third man, who was no longer in the flush of youth, dreamed only of eternal life. 'I do not want to die,' he thought. 'I want to live for ever.'

The fourth man, who had a wife and children to feed, dreamed only of being a great hunter. 'I do not ask for more,' he thought, 'than to see my family happy, healthy and well-fed.'

And so the four seekers climbed into their canoes and paddled them out into the sea, each man preoccupied with his own thoughts. But as they moved over the water, a wild wind came huffing and puffing about them, blowing them this way and that, battering their boats and threatening to drive them onto the rocks.

Then the first man took some tobacco and smoked it as a sacred offering. And the wind smelt the smell of the sweet smoke and was soothed and became calm.

The men paddled further out into the ocean. But the water grew dark and stormy and waves like rolling mountains heaved and tossed the canoes about like toy boats on a lake, like leaves bobbing on a stream, and were on the point of sinking them all.

Then the second man raised his voice in song. *Shuh-shuh ... shuh-shuh* ... be at peace. And the sea, bewitched by his song, was soothed and became calm.

The men paddled on. But a great white whale reared up out of the deep and thrashed about and whipped the sea to froth, threatening to overturn the canoes and drown their occupants.

Then the third man took out a whalebone charm which he carried on him. It was powerful medicine. He threw it into the water. And the whale, spellbound, was soothed and became calm.

The men paddled on. Now they could see the mists around Glooskap's island, but they could not see the island itself, so shrouded was it in billows of fog.

Then the fourth man took out his pipe and began to smoke, and the smoke he made parted the mist like a hand parting hair, and opened a pathway across the water.

There was Glooskap's island.

The four men beached their canoes and presented themselves before the great spirit.

'Please,' said the first man, bowing low, 'make me rich! I want wealth and power.'

'Please,' said the second, 'make me taller than any man! Then women will no longer laugh at me, and I can choose the most beautiful as my wife.'

'Please,' said the third, 'make me immortal. I want to live for all eternity.'

'Please' said the fourth, 'make me a great hunter. Then I will be able to feed my family.'

'Very well,' replied Glooskap. 'I grant you your wishes.' And he gave them each a small, buckskin pouch. 'In these bags are your hearts' desires. Do not open them until you are home.'

'We promise,' said the four men. And, clutching their gifts, they climbed into their canoes and began paddling back across the sea.

When they were in sight of land, the first man – who wished to exchange the burden of poverty for that of wealth – began to get curious. 'I wonder what *really* is in this bag? How can such a little thing contain all the possessions I wish for? We are nearly home after all – what harm would it do to take a little look ...'

Carefully, slowly, he untied the pouch.

It was as if he had released a herd of wild horses from a pen. Moose-skin hats and caribou-skin kilts and beaded capes and embroidered garters and belts and necklaces and armbands and leggings and moccasins and carved bone-handled knives and spears and baskets and cowhorn rattles and birch-bark boxes and bone dice spewed in tumbling torrents from the magic bag. They flowed into the canoe. They spilled out into the water. On and on, unstoppingly, the bag disgorged its treasure hoard until the canoe was so full and so heavily laden that it sank, taking the man with it.

The man who wished to be rich was drowned by the weight of his own wealth.

Meanwhile the second man – the one who wished to be tall – had arrived on the shore. Tucking his bag under his arm, he made for home.

But before he reached it, he, too, became curious. 'I think I will just take a little peek ...' he thought.

And he opened his pouch. *Whoosh!* His head, propelled by his expanding body, which was shooting upwards as fast as an arrow from a bow, was as high as the clouds. His legs fused together. He felt himself hardening, becoming rigid. He couldn't move. He was rooted to the spot.

The man who wished to be tall had become a tree, taller than all men.

The third man – the one who wanted eternal life – was almost home when his curiosity also got the better of him. 'Just a little look inside – then I'll close the bag and no one will be any the wiser ...'

And he, too, opened the pouch he had been given.

At once, a coldness seeped into his bones and his blood and a great heaviness weighed him down. If only he could just put this foot ... in front ... of ... the other. But he couldn't. He was frozen to the spot.

The man who wished to live forever had become a rock, which would last for all time.

The fourth man, meanwhile, had reached his home. His wife and children ran out to greet him. 'What have you brought? What is it – let us see!'

But the man – who wished to be a great hunter – waited until he was alone before he opened the pouch Glooskap had given him.

And as he did so, it was as if all the world was full of whispers – 'Here, Brother, we are here ...' It was the voices of the animals – the moose and the caribou, the seal, the beaver, the otter and the rabbit. They were calling to him and telling him where they were.

From that day on, the man never returned empty-handed from the hunt, and his family always had more than enough to eat. His wife, who had once been thin and hollow-cheeked, became plump and jolly; his children bloomed and flourished. As time passed, the man's increasing years were matched by his growing gratitude for all of life's bounty. And when he at last died, loved and respected by all, his spirit went to live in the Land of Souls.

As for the fog-bound island, it is still there. Drifts of mist coil around it like ghosts. The mist is the smoke from Glooskap's pipe.

COYOTE, FOX AND THE WOLVES

NEZ PERCÉ • PLATEAU AND BASIN

WORK, WORK, WORK. It was nothing but work, work, work from morning to night. Coyote was exhausted. First he had to hunt for his own food, and then he had to cook it himself! It really was too much. It had to stop.

'It's got to stop,' he said to Fox. 'Why should I have to slave away like this – me, Coyote? It just isn't right. You know what I need? A good man to look after me! Yes – that's the answer. I'm going to find myself a husband!'

'A husband?' Fox cried. 'How can you have a husband when you are a man?'

'Are you stupid as well as ugly?' replied Coyote. 'Must I explain everything to you? Of course I'm a man. But I'll *pretend* to be a woman.'

'But what about ... you know ... the wedding night?'

'Leave it all to me. I know what I'm doing. Now do you want to join me, or not?' Fox nodded reluctantly. 'Well, put this on – it should suit you.' And Coyote gave Fox a soft, fringed buckskin dress and a buckskin cape embroidered with beadwork stars. He put on a similar but even more magnificent costume himself.

'Perfect!' he said and gave a girlish giggle, just to get into practice.

And so it was, one fine day, that Coyote and Fox, disguised in women's clothing, set off to find themselves husbands.

Coyote knew just where to look. Not far away lived two wolf brothers who were renowned as great hunters. Coyote made straight for their lodge, with Fox trailing behind.

'Oh,' he cried tearfully as they drew near the two brothers who sat feasting on their latest catch, 'we are two lonely maidens wandering the wide, wide world in search of husbands. Where will we find them?'

The wolf brothers stopped eating. They looked the newcomers up and down. They saw their demure, downcast eyes. They took note of their firm bodies and full, feminine curves concealed behind their fringed buckskin dresses. Yes, they would make good wives – biddable yet strong, hard-working and fertile.

'I will marry you,' said Elder Brother Wolf to Coyote.

'I will marry you,' said Younger Brother Wolf to Fox.

'Come,' they said together, 'let us go to bed at once.'

'Just stop right there!' cried Coyote. 'Two gorgeous girls like us can't be too careful. How do we know that you will be good husbands – that you will take care of us, as husbands should? Before we agree to marry you, you will have to prove yourselves.

You have four days. If in that time you show yourselves to be skilled hunters who can bring home the meat, then – and only then – will we agree to marry you. And no scrappy little bits of lizard or vulture gristle, either – we want proper food!'

Thinking only of the moment when they could get their new brides into the marriage bed, the wolf brothers were happy to oblige.

They hunted as they had never hunted before. They brought back buffalo and elk and antelope and mountain sheep. They brought back salmon and wild goose. They brought back berries, roots, sweet herbs and honey.

They cooked as they had never cooked before. They stoked the fire and let the embers mellow to an ashen grey, and then they cooked the meat over it to melting, herb-flavoured readiness. They roasted the roots and served portions of berry-fruits and chunks of honeycomb. Nothing was too much trouble to please their brides-to-be.

'Scrape me some meat,' commanded Coyote, reclining back. 'There is a little left on the bone. I am too fatigued to do it myself.'

'Anything you say, my dearest,' said Elder Brother Wolf.

Coyote was in heaven. He had never enjoyed himself so much. He and Fox gorged themselves to the point of nausea. They had only to say 'Do it!' and it was done, so eager were their husbands-to-be to please them. The four days passed in an orgy of gluttony.

And then the fifth day came.

'Well, my dears,' said the wolf brothers. 'We have done as you asked. We have come to claim our reward.'

'Now you see what you've got us into!' hissed Fox at Coyote. 'You'd better get us out of it!'

'Leave it to me,' whispered Coyote. 'Yes, indeed,' he said to the wolves, 'you are great hunters and will make fine husbands. But before we come to bed, I must go and relieve myself. I want ...' and here there was much flirtatious giggling, 'to be truly ready for you.' And then he whispered to Fox again, 'When I say "run" – run!'

Coyote went outside. But he didn't go to relieve himself. Instead, he went to the lodge where the wolves' mother lay sleeping. He got into bed with her.

The wolves, meanwhile, were waiting impatiently. 'Your sister is taking her time,' they said to Fox.

Suddenly, the whole forest rang with a piercing 'Aaaah!' The wolves' mother had woken to find Coyote on top of her. Hearing her scream, the wolf brothers leapt up and raced to help her and to catch the one who had violated her.

'*Run-n-n-n!*' yelled Coyote. And Fox did. Coyote ran and Fox ran, and they ran and they ran and they ran, running for their lives, with the two howling wolves thundering after them. Beaded capes came off. Buckskin dresses came off. Fox and Coyote were as naked as the day they were born.

At last, the howling died away. The wolves had given up the chase. Fox and Coyote had escaped. They stopped to catch their breath.

'I won't try that again,' said Coyote.

'Nor will I,' said Fox.

Had they learnt their lesson? Who can say?

COYOTE AND THE EARTH MONSTER

FLATHEAD • PLATEAU AND BASIN

IT WAS A FINE DAY. Coyote was strolling along, humming a little tune.

'Where are you going?' a voice chirruped. It was Titmouse, perched on the branch of a tree.

'Here and there, this way and that,' replied Coyote.

'Well, take care where you walk. To the north there lives a giant monster who swallows up anyone who comes along.'

'How will I know him?'

'He is very big.'

'As big as a boulder?'

'Bigger.'

'As big as a hill?'

'Bigger.'

'As big as a mountain?'

'Bigger.'

'Tsch! Well, I'm not afraid of him. I won't fall into his trap – no, not me!'

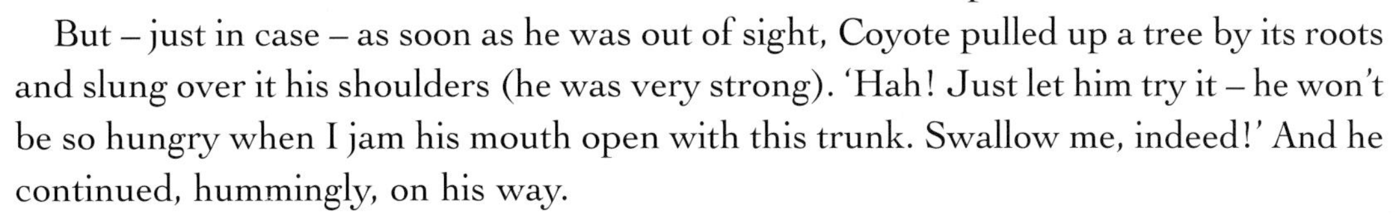

But – just in case – as soon as he was out of sight, Coyote pulled up a tree by its roots and slung over it his shoulders (he was very strong). 'Hah! Just let him try it – he won't be so hungry when I jam his mouth open with this trunk. Swallow me, indeed!' And he continued, hummingly, on his way.

He soon found himself in a vast canyon – or was it a cave? Tall red cliffs towered above him on either side. Their tops were so close together that not even a sliver of sky could be seen between them. And the canyon seemed to stretch forever. Coyote could not see where it ended.

And then his feet crunched on something. He looked down. The whole of the canyon floor was littered with bones. Human bones. What was this place – the valley of the dead?

'Help me,' cried a faint voice. 'Give me food. I'm starving to death.'

Coyote saw an old woman, as wasted as a skeleton. 'Here,' he said, offering her a piece of *pemmican* – dried meat pounded with fat and berries – which he kept on him.

The woman gulped the food down. 'Thank you,' she said. 'But tell me: why are you carrying a tree over your shoulders?'

'Aah,' said Coyote, 'that is to stop the monster swallowing me. I'll just wedge it into his mouth and he won't be able to shut it.'

'It's too late!' wailed the woman. 'He has already swallowed you. You are in his belly. He has closed his mouth, and there is no way out. No one ever leaves here. We are going to die, we are all going to die ...' And her wailing alerted hundreds of other souls who came crawling and dragging themselves along the canyon floor, too weak to stand – the cadaverous, skeletal, living dead.

Coyote looked back to the entrance of the canyon. What the old woman had said was true: the opening was sealed.

'Well,' he said. 'I don't know what you're all complaining about. This place is full of food! If we are inside the monster's belly, then the sides of the canyon must be his flesh.' And he sliced off some of the lining of the monster's stomach and shared it out. 'How about some liver? Or a little kidney?'

The starving people gorged themselves on the monster's body. Its blood quenched their thirst. Its meat made them strong.

Far away, Coyote could hear a drumming sound. *Thrumm, thrumm,* it went. He decided to investigate. He began to explore. *Thrumm, thrumm*. The drumming was getting louder: he must be getting closer.

And then Coyote saw it. A vast, throbbing, pulsating thing as big as a mountain.

It was the monster's heart.

Coyote took out the knife he carried in his belt. He plunged it deep into the heart. Again he plunged it and again, slicing and slashing and hacking.

With a mighty explosion that shook the universe, the heart burst, disgorging a torrent of thick, treacly, red-hot liquid, like lava from a volcano.

'Quick!' screamed Coyote, 'run!'

As the earth monster writhed and shuddered in its death throes and the whole world trembled, the people made for its mouth, which was now opening and shutting wildly as it gasped for air.

'Quick! This way!'

At last, everyone was out. Except, that is, for one small creature, which had become stuck in the dying monster's closing mouth. It was Woodtick.

'Come on,' said Coyote, 'I'll pull you out.' And he took hold of Woodtick's front legs and pulled. *Ooh, aah,* just one more time ... what a tight squeeze ... now breathe in ... that's it, nearly done.

At last! Woodtick was free. But all the pulling and the squashing and the squeezing had changed his shape. Where once he had been round, now he was flat. Woodtick went off to hide in the mountain woods where he has lived ever since, waiting to suck the blood of the animals and people that pass by.

Perhaps Coyote should have left him behind.

COYOTE AND THE BOX OF LIGHT

ZUNI • SOUTHWEST

IF THERE WAS ONE THING COYOTE DID NOT LIKE, it was hard work. If he could trick someone else into doing his chores, he would. He was the laziest creature alive.

One day Coyote saw Eagle. He was hunting, swooping down on rabbits and snatching them up before they even realized he was there. One, two, three, four. He caught more rabbits in a day than Coyote did in a week. Coyote was impressed.

'Brother Eagle!' he called. 'Please, *please* stop! You are working yourself too hard. Let me help you ... two can do twice as much as one.'

Eagle agreed, and so the pair began hunting together. But it was an uneven partnership. For every three rabbits Eagle caught, Coyote caught only the odd grub. But when the time came to divide up the catch, they each got equal shares. Coyote made quite sure of that.

'Oh,' he complained, 'you know I would bring in more if I could. But how can I hunt when I can hardly see? It is just so dark! If only I had more light, I'd show you what I can do.' And it was indeed very dark, for all this happened in the days before the Sun and Moon were in the sky.

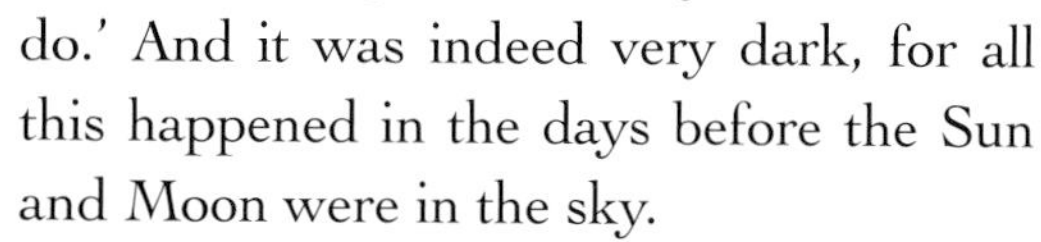

Eagle took Coyote at his word. 'I know where there is light,' he said. 'In the west. Let us go there.' Coyote had to agree, and so the pair set off. Eagle was able to soar over the mountains and valleys and rivers that they had to cross. But Coyote, being earth-bound, had to walk. His feet were sore, his legs ached, his fur was caked with mud, and he was thoroughly fed up. Why hadn't he kept his mouth shut?

At last they reached the west, where Eagle said the light was. And there, in a pueblo village, they saw *kachinas* – spirits – dancing.

'Come,' said the people gathered to watch the sacred dance, 'come and join us.' And they made the pair welcome and plied them with food and drink.

Coyote looked around him. In a corner there were two boxes. Every now and then, someone would open one of them and light would shine out. They opened the boxes in turn, first one, then the other. The glow that came from the smaller one was cool and silver. The glare from the larger one was blindingly bright, like fire. So that's where the light was hidden, thought Coyote.

'Psst,' he whispered to Eagle, 'over here! They keep the light in these boxes. But they'll never give them to us – we'll have to steal them.'

That was how Coyote turned Eagle into a thief.

The pair waited until the kachinas had left and the people had gone to their homes. Then Eagle swooped down, quickly emptied the contents of the smaller box into the larger, tucked the larger box under his wing and flew off, with Coyote loping behind him, breathlessly trying to keep up.

'Brother Eagle …' puffed Coyote, 'let me carry the box for you.'

'No,' said Eagle, 'you would drop it.' And he flew on.

'Brother Eagle …' persisted Coyote, 'let me carry the box for you.'

'No,' said Eagle, 'you would lose it.' And he flew on.

'Brother Eagle …' the whining voice drifted up again, 'let me carry the box for you.'

'No,' said Eagle, 'you would break it.' And he flew on.

'Brother Eagle …'

'Oh, all right then! Here – catch!' And Eagle dropped the box down to Coyote who stood, panting, below.

Coyote hung back while Eagle flew on ahead. When the big bird was out of sight, he slowly lifted the lid of the box to peep inside.

The lid blew off. Out flew the Moon and rose into the sky. The world was lit by a cool, silver light, and it became cold, very cold.

Out flew the Sun and disappeared over the far horizon. The sky grew dark, the plants withered, and all the leaves dropped from the trees.

'Wait, wait!' called Coyote. 'Come back! I only wanted to have a little look.' But he could not put the Sun and the Moon back into the box.

Eagle, meanwhile, had returned to see what was taking Coyote so long.

'You stupid animal – what have you done?' he shouted angrily when he saw the box lying open and empty on its side. 'Don't you know that you have let cold and winter into the world? If it weren't for your foolishness, we would have summer all year round.'

Coyote hung his head in shame. But what he had done couldn't be undone.

So it was that winter came into the world, and so it has been ever since.

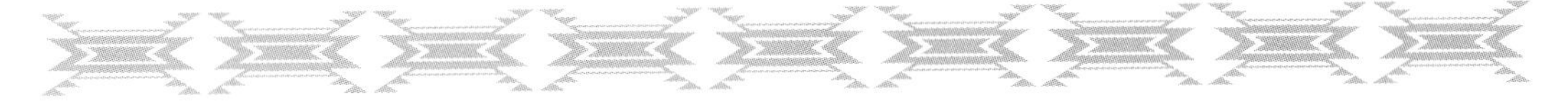

EARTH, SEA AND SKY

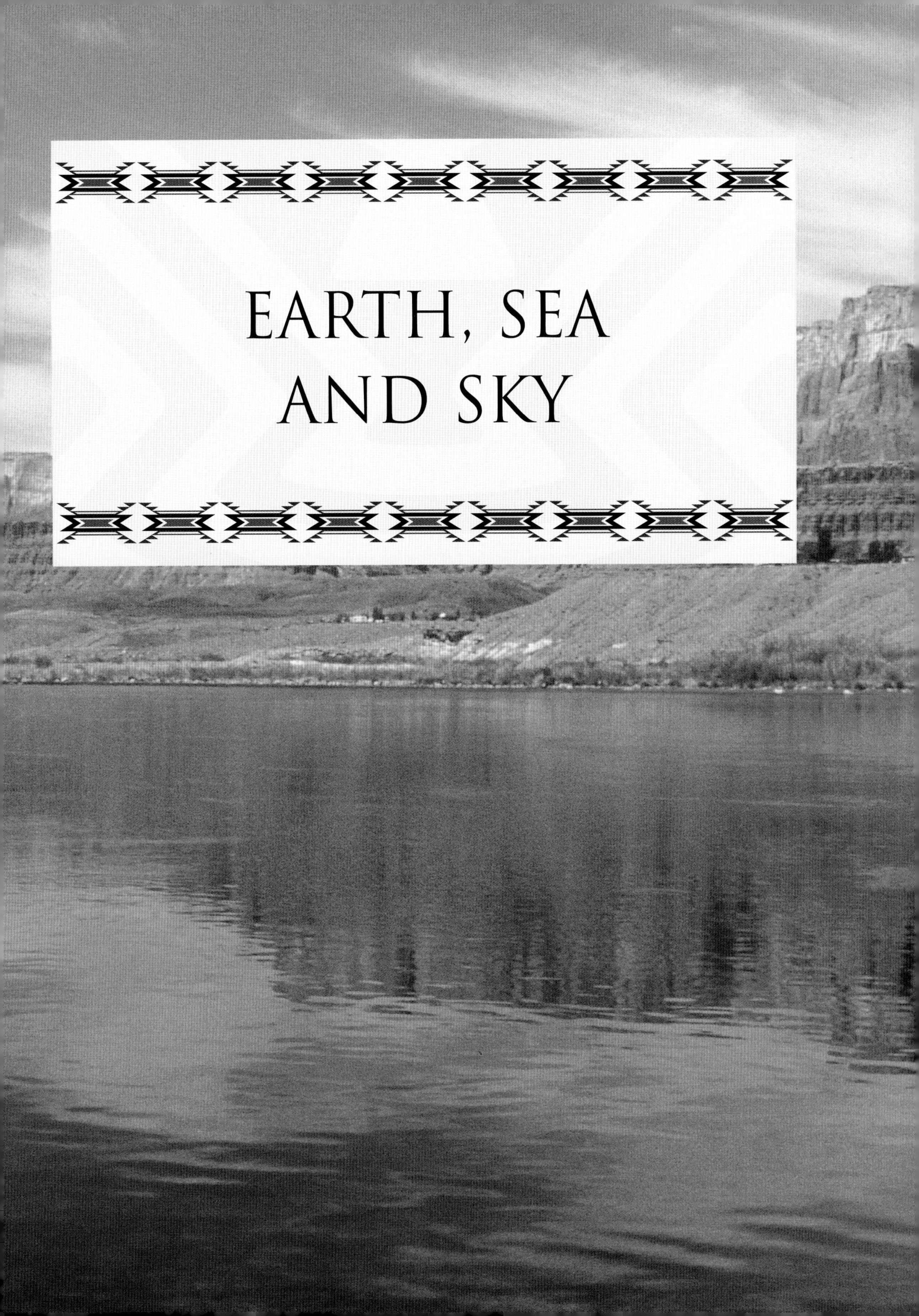

Thunderbird and the Water Monster

SIOUX • PLAINS

The lightning is the flash of his eye.
The thunder is the boom of his voice.
You cannot see him for he is wrapped in cloud.
He is *Wakinyan Tanka.*
He is the Great Thunderbird.

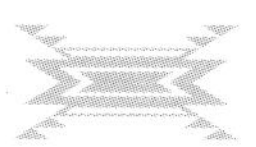

Long, long ago, before the time we are living in now, a terrible thing happened to the world. The people who survived it did not forget. And so that others should not forget either, the people took the memory of what had happened and put it into a story and gave the story to their children. The children passed it on to their children and so, in this way, the story was handed on down through the generations. Of course, it did not stay exactly the same over all this time. A detail was added here, an alteration made there, so that as the years went by the story evolved and reformed, like a drifting cloud swelling and shrinking.

As the world slowly changed, people stopped believing in the truth of the story. 'That's just an old legend, a fantasy, a fairy tale,' they said. But those among us who are wiser and less proud imagine otherwise. We know that deep in the heart of the story is an ancient memory. And we know that the memory is true.

This is the story as it has come down to us.

The Great Unktehi was a huge, ugly monster. She had scales like a snake, feet like a frog, and horns and a tail that she could push out or pull in, like a snail. She lived in the Missouri River. Her long, sinuous body followed every curve of its course, filling it from source to mouth. Her babies, the little Unktehi, lived in the tributaries to the sides.

The Great Unktehi hated the human race. 'What are they good for, these little worms, these scraps of life? They are so puny they do not even make a good meal. I will get rid of them all!'

So she puffed up her body to make the river overflow its banks, and spewed a torrent of water out of her mouth. The little Unktehi did the same, in their own little way. The land was flooded and many people drowned. A few managed to escape into the hills.

From his home in the sacred *Pa Sapa*, the Black Hills, Wakinyan Tanka, the Great Thunderbird, looked out over the world. He saw what was happening.

'I must stop this destruction or there will be no humans left.' His voice rumbled over the prairie like the unfurling of a mighty blanket.

He called together his brothers, the other Thunderbirds, and his children. 'Come, my brothers, my little eaglets, it is time to go to war.'

The Wakinyan went down to the rivers and the land, and a terrible battle began. The Thunderbirds attacked their enemies with their teeth and their claws, and the water monsters lashed back with their spiked tails. When they saw that the monsters were winning, the Thunderbirds withdrew to their own territory, the mountains and the sky. But it was only to consider a new strategy.

'They are creatures of earth and water,' said Wakinyan Tanka, 'we of fire and air. Let us fight with weapons more suited to our nature.'

And so, enveloped in war-clothes of cloud, the Thunderbirds returned to battle wielding thunderbolts and lightning darts. One bolt after another they let fly, dart after dart. The black and shuddering sky was alight with a thousand arrows of fire. They fell to Earth, setting the forests alight, drying up the streams and rivers, and burning up the Unktehi until there was nothing left of them but bare bones.

Up in the hills where they had taken refuge, the people saw that the monsters were dead. They came down and looked about them at the altered world, and gazed in amazement at the skeletons of the terrible creatures who had caused so much destruction, lying there where they had fallen in the contorted throes of death. Then they set about making new lives for themselves, building homes and having children and grandchildren and great-grandchildren.

In the place where all of this happened, the bones of the Unktehi may still be seen. They are the rocks and hills of *Mako Sicha*, the Badlands of South Dakota.

WHY THE SUN HIDES FROM THE MOON

INUIT • ARCTIC

SHE DID NOT KNOW WHO HE WAS, the man who forced her, for it was too dark to see. The wind had blown the lamps out and there was no other light – in those days, it was always night.

The first time it happened, she was taken by surprise. But the second time, she was ready for him. She smeared her hands with soot from the fire and placed them on his back. When the lamps were relit, she looked for the man whose back bore her mark.

She saw him.

It was her own brother.

She was horrified. 'It is against nature! Against the laws by which we live!' How can you have done this terrible thing?' And she ran off into the blackness, a blazing torch in her hand.

Picking up another torch, her brother followed her. But in his haste, he tripped and fell. His torch went out.

A big wind lifted the sister and her brother into the sky. With her shining torch still in her hand, she became the Sun. With no torch to dazzle with, he became the Moon.

Sister Sun keeps well away from Brother Moon. When she sees his pale face peering above the horizon, she slips behind the western edge of the world and stays hidden until the night is over and he has gone. When he is on one side of the sky, she is on the other. She keeps this distance between them always.

So it was and so it is, from that day to this.

Father Sun and the Twin Boys

NAVAJO • SOUTHWEST

Earth Mother, Changing Woman, *Estanatlehi* – it is she who is our mother, she who made us from cornmeal and water and skin from her own breast. Changing Woman is beautiful, too, so beautiful that one day the Sun came down to woo her. He caressed her with sunbeams, lighter than the touch of a feather. He suffused her with warmth. And the result nine months later, of this coupling of Earth and Sky, was a pair of twin baby boys.

In the time when this happened, the world was full of monsters and giants who had a taste for human flesh. One such roamed the country near where the boys and their mother lived.

To their *hogan*, their earth hut, the giant came one day. He sniffed the air like a hound on the scent. 'Is that smell what I think it is? Human flesh? Infant flesh? Tell me, my dear, are there any *children* here?'

'No, no. No children at all! Absolutely none,' said Changing Woman, standing on the stone over the hole in the earth in which she had hidden her twins.

But the giant did not give up so easily. 'My nose rarely deceives me – I know the aroma of baby-meat when I smell it. If there are no children here, what, then, are those footprints in the dust?'

'Those? Oh, those! You have discovered my little foolishness. I am, you see, childless. To comfort me in my loneliness, I make the footprints myself – like this, you see,' and she pressed the palms of her hands and the tips of her fingers into the dust, 'and then I pretend they are the marks of my own little ones.'

'Aah, now I understand,' said the giant, almost convinced but not entirely.

As the twins grew, it became more and more difficult to keep them hidden. It also became increasingly difficult to avoid their persistent questions.

'Who is our father?' they asked.

'Nobody ...'

'But we must have a father. Who is he?'

'The Sun ...'

'The *Sun!* And where does he live?'

'Nowhere and everywhere ...'

'No, tell us. He must live somewhere. Where is it?'

'Oh, far, far away. In the east.'

'Then we will go to find him.'

And so the twins, who were by now strong and handsome young men, armed

themselves with bows and arrows and set off to find their father.

Over plains and rivers they went, through swamps and deltas and creeks. But the Sun was not in the east.

'Mother, you have lied to us. Where does our father live?'

'He lives in the south.'

Over peaks and through valleys they went, through jungle and cloud forest. But the Sun was not in the south.

'Mother, you have lied to us. Where does our father live?'

'He lives in the north.'

Over mountains and vast forests they went, across lakes and over ice. But the Sun was not in the north.

'Mother, you have lied to us. Where does our father live?'

'He lives in the west.'

Over desert and scrubland they went, over ridges and through ravines. But the Sun was not in the west.

'Mother, you have lied to us. Where does our father live?'

'Yes, my sons, I have lied to you. Your father the Sun lives far, far away, on the other side of the Big Water. But you will never reach him. There are too many obstacles in your path. There are the clapping rocks that will crush you. There are the reeds with edges like knives that will tear your skin. There is the canyon that is so deep it will swallow you whole. And then there is the Big Water which no man can cross.'

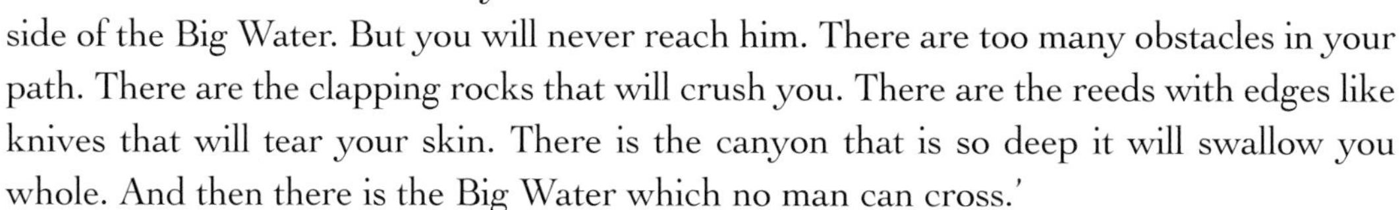

'Then that,' said the twins, undeterred, 'is the road we shall take.'

It was useless to stop them; their mother could see that. So she taught them a magic song for their protection:

We are walking,
We are walking
To seek the Sun, our father.

She told them to sing the song four times whenever danger was nearby. Then she sent them on their way.

Singing, singing, singing, they walked – one day, two days, three. Now it was the fourth day and they were travelling along a dusty track between strange rocks which rose like petrified giants on either side of them.

'Come here, come here, come here,' called a voice. 'Come here,' it said again.

They looked around. There was no one there.

'Climb up, climb up, climb up,' it said. 'Climb up,' it said again.

The brothers stared up. The voice was coming from the top of a tall column of stone called Spider Rock. It was Old Lady Eight-legs talking to them, Grandmother Spider.

'Your tower is too steep, Grandmother. We cannot climb.' But as they looked up, a fine rope of spider's silk was lowered towards them. They took hold of the end of it and pulled themselves up.

At the top of the column the Grandmother sat at her loom. Around her were parcels of bones bound in spider's silk, the remains of the wicked whom she had killed .

'Good-day to you, Grandmother,' they said.

'And good-day to you, my grandsons,' she replied. 'I know where you are going, and why. But there are dangers on the road. I will teach you songs to keep you safe, and I will give you this, too,' and she handed them each a feather. 'Hold up these feathers in the face of danger and all danger will melt away.'

'Thank you, Grandmother Spider,' said the twins. And with the songs in their souls and the feathers in their hands, they lowered themselves down the silk rope, and continued their journey.

Days and weeks went by. And then it happened again – a voice calling to them from nowhere.

'Psst,' it whispered. The twins looked around. There was no one to be seen.

'Down here,' it said. The voice was coming from the ground. As the brothers watched, the dry, sandy soil beneath their feet parted and out came a strange-looking little creature with eight legs, a red head and a stripy back. It was Scorpion Man.

He dusted the sand off his legs and shook himself. 'Good-day, my sons,' he said. 'I know where you are going, and why. Now do as I tell you ...'

The brothers did as he instructed them. They placed their hands on the ground, spat into them four times, then closed their fists on the spittle.

'Do not wash your hands until you come to the Big Water,' said Scorpion Man.

'We promise,' said the brothers, and went on their way.

The road was long and the road was hard, and days and weeks went by. And then the twins came to the first of the dangers – the clapping rocks, waiting to crush them as they walked in-between. But, chanting the songs they had learnt –

We are walking,
We are walking

To seek the Sun, our father

– they held out their feathers in front of them and the rocks stopped, as if holding their breath, to let the brothers through.

The road was long and the road was hard, and days and weeks went by. And then the brothers came to the second danger – the reeds with edges like knives that would tear their skin. Chanting their songs as before – *We are walking, we are walking* – they lightly touched the reeds with their feathers and the reeds instantly turned into catkins. So pleased were they with their transformation that they parted in the middle, as if in a broad smile, to let the twins through.

The road was long and the road was hard, and days and weeks went by. But finally the two brothers came to the third danger – the canyon that was so deep that it would swallow them whole. They could see no way across. But they lifted up their voices and sang the songs that their mother had taught them, that Spider Woman had taught them – *We are walking, we are walking* – and all at once a rainbow appeared in the sky, spanning the ravine. The brothers stepped onto the rainbow bridge and walked safely over the gorge of the Colorado River that white men call the Grand Canyon.

Now there was only the Big Water to cross.

And there, at last, it was. It stretched so far that the twins could not imagine how they would ever reach the other side. But they had passed through all three dangers. They would overcome this one, too.

So they did as Scorpion Man had instructed. Singing and praying, they washed the spittle off their hands. At once, an iridescent arc of colours appeared in the sky, glowing, intensifying – the rainbow!

The twins placed their feet on heaven's bridge and they walked and they walked and they walked all the way over the Big Water to the Sun's house behind the sea.

'Welcome, welcome, my sons, a thousand, thousand welcomes,' said the Sun. And father and sons, meeting for the first time, embraced.

Armed by their father with knives made of stone and sundarts and arrows of lightning, the twins later returned to the world and became great heroes, killing giants and destroying monsters and making the world a safer place for humankind. And their mother, when she saw this, was proud of them, so proud.

In his turquoise house in the east, the Sun readies himself for the journey.
Which mount shall it be for today?
A fine-weather filly, of turquoise, of white shell, of pearl?

Or a storm-steed, of red shell, or swarthy coal?
Placing his gold disc on his back, he climbs onto his chosen beast
and begins the long ride from east to west.
The hooves of his horse stir up sky-dust –
the god's sacred pollen given in homage.
It looks like gold mist on the horizon.
Saddle-sore, the Sun arrives at his house in the west.
He is weary after lighting the world.
He hangs his gold disc on its peg to cool.
Until tomorrow, which is another day.

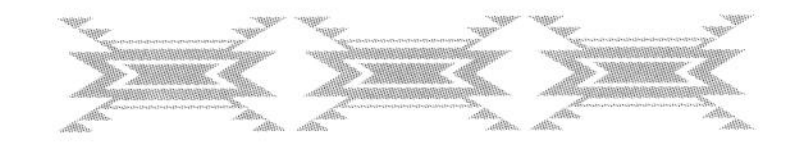

How Spider Stole the Sun

CHEROKEE • SOUTHEAST

In the beginning, it was so dark that the animals could hardly see anything at all. They kept bumping into each other.

'Watch where you're going – that's my tail!' yelled Snake.

'Ouch! You stepped on my foot!' shouted Fox.

'Get out of my way,' roared Bear, 'or I'll crush you all!'

It was no good. They couldn't go on like this. All they had was the Moon whose glimmer was weak and cold. They would have to get light from somewhere else.

And then Owl remembered. 'I know where the light is!' he cried. 'On the other side of the world. Those people over there are keeping it all to themselves. It's time we had some, too! I will go and steal a bit from them.'

Owl flew off to the far side of the world – and there was the light he wanted. A great, big, burning ball of radiance, wedged between the branches of a tree. It was so dazzling that it lit up the whole sky. He gathered a little piece in his talons.

Ooh! Aah! Whoo-whoo! It was red-hot. Owl flipped the spark of brightness from one foot to the other and tossed it from wing to wing. He couldn't keep hold of it ... a second ... longer. He made such a fuss and commotion that he alerted the people who owned the light. They came running, snatched the spark back, and chased Owl away. Empty-taloned, he returned to the other animals.

The experience left Owl scarred. His pristine white feathers – of which he had been

very proud – were now smudged and streaked and charred where the spark had burnt them. They would never be the same again.

Ever since then, Owl has had an aversion to light and comes out only in darkness.

As for the other animals, they were no better off than before. They were still groping around in the dark. No, it was no good. Someone else would have to try to steal the light.

'I'll go!' volunteered Opossum. And she set off on the long journey. Being unable to fly, it took her longer than Owl. But at last she arrived – and there was the light, a great, big, burning ball of radiance, still wedged between the branches of the tree. Laboriously, Opossum climbed up and, with her sharp claws, broke off a little piece.

Ooh! Aah! Ouch! It was red-hot. Quickly she coiled her long, densely furred tail around to form a pocket, dropped the spark into it, and began to make her way home.

She didn't notice anything at first. But then the smell of burning reached her nostrils. She looked around. Her tail – her pride and joy – was smoking.

Help! She dropped the spark at once. And the noise alerted the owners of the light who came running to chase the thief away, just as they had done Owl.

Opossum looked at her tail, which had once been so lush and beautiful. All the hairs on it were blackened and singed and, as she watched, they fell out – one by one. It was a hideous sight. Her tail was bald! She felt deeply embarrassed.

Ever since then Opossum has had an aversion to light and comes out only in darkness.

After this, various other animals tried to do what Owl and Opossum had failed to do – Fox, Buzzard, Raven – but all were equally unsuccessful.

'Let me try,' piped a small, quavering voice. It was old Lady Eight-Legs, Grandmother Spider.

First she made a large pot which she placed on her back. Then, on the end of a silken thread as diaphanous as air and as strong as iron, she dropped down to the other side of the world. Working fast with all her eight little legs, she manoeuvred the burning ball of light into the bowl. Then she pulled herself back to where she had started along her silk thread, her lifeline – and all so quickly and silently that it was some time before the owners of the light realized what had happened.

Back home, Grandmother Spider released the light from her pot – and the Sun rose in the sky.

Ever since then the Sun has not stayed on one side of the world. It rises in the east and travels to the west so that all the Earth's creatures can have their share of its glorious light.

WOMEN'S WORK

As in so many cultures worldwide, the spider – or Spider Woman in the case of the Native Americans – was the Spinning Goddess who imparted her knowledge of spinning and weaving to humankind, crafts which are seen as primarily female.

Along the Northwest Coast, Tlingit, Tsimshian and Haida women used the wool of mountain goats and cedar bark fibre to weave the famous Chilkat blankets, which were worn by high-ranking individuals at ceremonies such as the *potlatch*. In the same region, Salish weavers added the hair of small, domesticated dogs to their basic stock. In the Southwest, Pueblo women were weaving cloth from cotton fibre long before the arrival of the first Europeans. The Navajo, who learned their weaving skills from the Pueblos, produced and continue to produce their renowned blankets and rugs with their distinctive patterns, including images of the Yeibechi spirits which feature in ancient Navajo sandpaintings.

The Nez Percé of the Plateau region were famous for their 'cornhusk bags' – flat bags made by twining hemp cord (or willow or elderberry bark fibre). During this process, cornhusk or grass fibre or, later, coloured yarn, was intertwined to produce a pattern. In California, Pomo women produced baskets so tightly woven they could hold water.

In the Southeast, women were so adept at weaving plant fibres that the first white settlers thought they were using cotton yarn. In this same region, Seminole women were to become famous for their patchwork, made from calico, coloured cloth and ribbons acquired from European traders in the late nineteenth century.

On the Plains, women applied their creative skills to another material in plentiful supply: animal hide. Dressing the skin of a buffalo, deer, antelope or bighorn sheep was a woman's job, and the quality and quantity of skins she treated was a reflection of her ability and worth. First, she used special tools to clean the hide of fat, tissue and hair. Then she stretched it out on the ground or on a wooden frame, and rubbed an oily mixture of fat, brains and liver into it. She left it to dry in the sun, washed it, rubbed it and finally stretched it again. The result, if she had done her job properly, was a fine hide, soft enough for clothing.

While the leatherworkers of the Plains were dressing animal skins, their counterparts in the far Arctic were fashioning weather-cheating garments of seal or caribou skin, or cutting dried seal intestines into strips to make ingenious waterproof clothing.

SEDNA AND THE SEA

INUIT • ARCTIC

IN THE TIME WHEN ANYTHING COULD HAPPEN AND OFTEN DID – when forests grew at the bottom of the ocean, when snow could catch fire and houses could fly – there lived a girl called Sedna. Sedna was young and Sedna was pretty and more men wanted to marry her than you could count on the fingers of both hands. 'Be my wife …' 'I will give you whatever you wish …' 'See how handsome I am …' 'See how rich …' But Sedna was deaf to all their pleas.

One day, a handsome stranger came to woo her. He came from the sea. He was dressed in furs and in his hand he carried an ivory spear. He did not set foot on the shore but instead stood in his kayak, rocking on the restless water. Above the whooshing of the waves and the soughing of the wind, Sedna heard him singing –

Come away, come away with me
To the land of birds
Where there is no hunger
Where you will sleep in bearskins
Where the oil-lamp will always burn
And the stewpot be always full.

– or perhaps it was only the crying of the sea birds, wheeling overhead.

The next day the stranger came again … *Come away, come away with me* … and the next day, and the next, and Sedna found herself gradually falling under his spell.

And so it was, early one morning when no one else was awake, that she arose from her warm bed, gathered a few possessions, left her home and her father who had been her only parent since her mother died, and ran down to the shore where her lover

waited, rocking in his kayak on the restless sea.

The pair set off across the water, her lover skilfully guiding the craft between drifting blocks of ice over the tilting, pitching, iron-dark waves. But they had not gone far – barely out of sight of land – when a change began to come over him. All the features that had marked him out as human faded ... mouth and nose and hands and feet evaporated, like trails of mist, leaving the man Sedna had run away with as he truly was: a phantom, a spirit-being whose natural form was that of a sea-bird, a petrel or a loon, as the mood took him.

Sedna was in despair. She looked back across the sea to the tiny black ridges along the horizon which she knew to be her homeland. She would never see it again. She burst into tears and cried and cried and cried.

When her father discovered that Sedna had gone, and realized with whom, he set off to bring her back. By luck or skill, he at last reached the land of birds where she now lived. By luck or good timing, her bird-husband was away when he arrived.

Quickly, her father lifted Sedna up and carried her to his kayak, waiting on the shore. He tucked her into one of the hatches, covered her with furs to keep her warm, climbed into the other hatch, and set off in the direction in which he had come.

Splash and dip, dip and splash went the paddle as the little boat cut through the waves, making desperately for home.

Splash and dip, dip and splash went the paddle as the bird-spirit, in his human form, closed in on them from behind.

'Let me see her! Let me see my wife!' he called.

But her father covered Sedna with furs to hide her.

'Go away! You will never see her again!'

With a wail of despair, the bird-spirit changed into a loon, spread his wings and took to the air, his eerie cry echoing over the water.

His cry awoke the sleeping sea, raising it to a storm. Rough waves lashed at the kayak, licking hungrily at its sides, drooling over its deck, longing to swallow it up.

'It wants her – the sea wants her ...' thought Sedna's panic-stricken father. 'If I do not give the sea what it craves, it will drown us both. The bird-man has won, and I have lost.'

And so terror made the father do what he thought he never could. He leaned over, pulled his daughter from her seat, and gave her to the waves.

'FATHER!' she screamed. 'Save me! Save me!' And her desperate hands grappled for the side of the boat.

The father could not bear it. He must make this quick. And he brought down his ivory axe – *smash*! – on the fingers clinging for life to the kayak.

UNDERSEA JOURNEYS

In his definitive work on the subject, *Shamanism: Archaic techniques of ecstasy*, Mircea Eliade gives a detailed description of the journey of an Inuit shaman, or *angakok*, to visit the Mother of the Sea Beasts, known as *Takanakapsaluk*. The *angakok* may undertake the journey to retrieve the stolen soul of an individual who has, as a result of the theft, become sick. Alternatively, if hunting has been poor and starvation threatens, either for an individual or the community, he will travel to the home of the Sea Mother to ask her to release the animals she has been withholding. Only his spirit makes the journey: his physical body remains behind, bound with ropes to prevent it disappearing, too.

When the *angakok* is acting for the community, the event is a communal one. All the villagers gather to help him on his way, and sit in silence with eyes closed. Breathing deeply, the *angakok* enters a state of ecstatic trance and begins to summon his spirit helpers. 'The way is opening for me,' he murmurs as he sees them arrive, and the spectators, in call-and-response fashion, reply, 'Let it be so.' As the way opens fully, the shaman has to fight forces which only he can see. During his struggle, the audience continue chanting and dead shamans, come to give their assistance, reveal their presence by their sighing and breathing. The spectators know that the shaman is no longer with them when his cries can no longer be heard.

Down at the bottom of the sea, the *angakok* has to overcome certain obstacles before he can stand in front of *Takanakapsaluk* – moving rocks which threaten to crush him; a dog with bared teeth which blocks his way; the Sea Mother's own father who, mistaking the visitor for a dead man, attempts to seize him and take him to the land of ghosts. Sometimes there may also be a high wall which the goddess has raised in front of her house as a sign of her displeasure with humans; to achieve entry, the shaman must knock this down with his shoulder. Sometimes, however, her house is roofless so that she can get a better view of human activities from her seat by the fire.

In her anguish over the wrongdoings of people, the Sea Mother has become dirty and unkempt, and she has penned up the sea mammals in a pool to the right of the fire. The *angakok's* task is to comb her hair while trying to persuade her to release the imprisoned creatures. When he succeeds, the spectators back on earth hear the animals moving out into the water and see the shaman 'surface' from the sea, gasping for breath.

The severed tips bobbed away on the water and turned into seals.

'FATHER!' called the girl again, reaching for the boat with her mutilated hands. 'Help me! I am drowning!'

Her pale face rose and fell with the swell of the waves. She belonged to the sea – why would she not surrender? Why was she prolonging the horror? Why, thought the father, couldn't she just go ahead and *drown*?

Again the father raised his axe. *Hack, hack!* He sliced off what was left of her fingers, which floated away to become walruses. And again! *Chop, chop* – he severed her hands at the wrists, and they floated away to become whales.

Having nothing left to hold on with, poor Sedna relinquished herself to her fate as the sea closed over her, wrapping her its rocking embrace and dragging her down.

Then all was still and peaceful once more, as if no struggle had ever occurred. And the father paddled for home, bearing a burden of guilt that he would carry for the rest of his days.

But that was not the end of Sedna, for she became the Spirit of the Sea. She is Takanaksaluk, the Terrible-One-Down-There. She is *Immap Ukuua*, the Mother of the Sea. All the sea mammals are her children. The seals (her fingertips) are hers; the walruses (her fingers) are hers; the whales (her hands) are hers. When hunters violate her rules, she withholds her animals or raises storms so that no one can venture onto the water. Then the holy men, the shamans, have to sea-travel to visit her. Down in the depths of the ocean, they comb her hair which, having no hands, she cannot comb herself, and ask her to forgive the wrongdoings of humankind.

As for Sedna's father, it is said that he drowned. On the night he returned, a freak tide rose and carried away the tent in which he slept and in which Sedna's dog lay, tied up in the *tupik*, the tent. Ever since then, man and dog have lived beneath the water in a place called Adliden, where souls come after death to atone for the sins of the living.

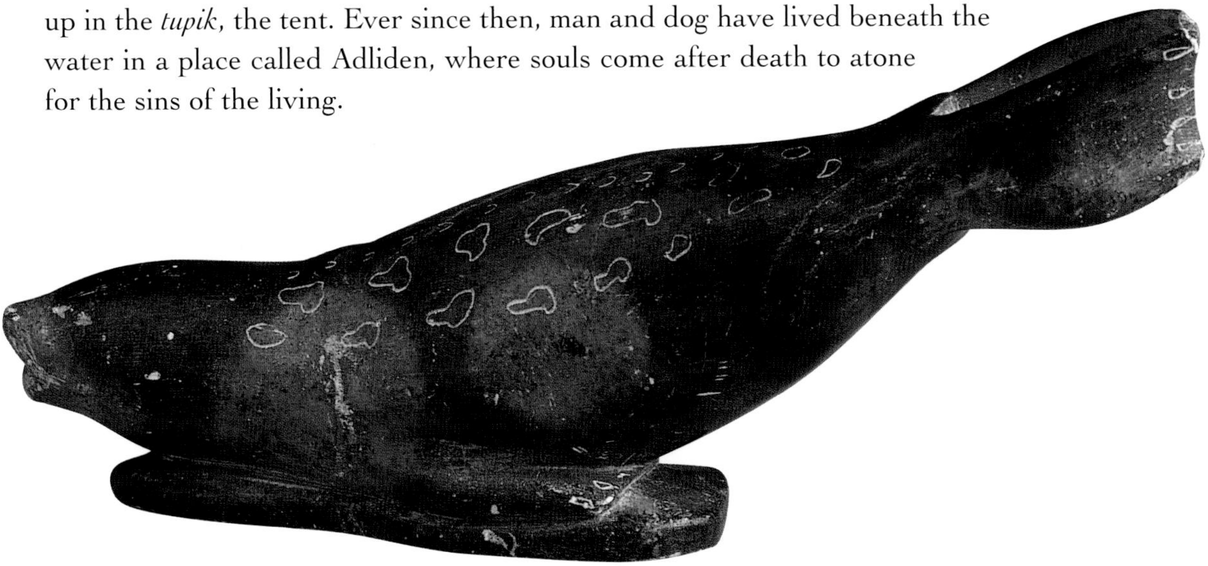

WHY NIGHT FOLLOWS DAY

BLACKFEET • PLAINS

THERE WAS ONCE A MAN WHO HAD A WIFE AND TWO SONS. The man had little luck in hunting so the family was forced to survive on a diet of roots and berries. It was a meagre existence.

Then one day the man had a dream. In the dream a voice spoke to him.

'Look to the spider,' it said, 'and see how she hunts her prey.'

Well, thought the man, anything was worth a try. So he found the largest spider's web he could and carefully detached it, line by line, from its anchor points. He spread it out between the trees, across the trail which the animals used. And then he waited.

In no time at all, the web was sagging with the weight of deer, rabbits and other game tangled, as if by magic, in its barely visible but sticky threads. And so it went on, the next day and the next and the day after that, too. Now the man and his family had all they wanted to eat, and life was good.

But it was not to last. As the man was returning home early from collecting his catch one day, he caught sight of his wife perfuming herself with sweet pine which she was burning on the fire. 'Hmm,' he brooded, 'such beautification is not for my benefit! She must have a lover.' And so he decided to spy on her, to uncover the truth for himself.

The next day he found a deer caught in his web. He killed the animal, cut up some of the meat, but left the carcass behind, and returned home. There was his wife.

'Ooh,' he complained, 'this deer-meat was so heavy I could hardly carry it. I have had to leave the bones behind. Please fetch them for me. I cannot walk another step.'

His wife got up and set off in the direction of the web. But she was no fool. She knew he was suspicious. So, when she had reached the top of the nearest hill, she turned back as if to wave goodbye – really she wanted to see if he was following her. But no. There he was, still sitting – puffing and exhausted – where she had left him. She waved and he waved back. Then she disappeared over the crest of the hill and out of sight.

Instantly the man got up. He went to his children. 'Where does your mother go in the day, when I am out hunting?' he asked them.

Two little fingers pointed in the same direction. 'Over there. To those dead trees over there. She goes to see the Snake-man.'

So that was it! His wife was infatuated with – of all things – a snake! Well, supernatural being or not, he would put a stop to it, right now. He marched over to

the trees and poked and prodded about until at last he uncovered a den of rattlesnakes. He wasted no time. Piling up some dry sticks, he kindled a fire. The fire caught the dry wood of the trees. The trees burst into flame. And before you could say 'snake in the grass', the entire clump and its inhabitants were reduced to cinders.

The man returned to his children. 'When your mother comes back she will be very angry. So you must run away. Here – take these – they will help to keep you safe.' And he gave his sons a stick, a stone, and a handful of wet moss.

Then he spread his spider's web over the opening to the lodge and sat down to wait for the return of his wife. He did not have to wait long. She had seen the blaze of the burning trees from a distance away and, suspecting the worst, came running back.

'What have you done?' she yelled. 'Where are you? Come on out – I know you're in there!' And in attempting to enter the lodge where she thought her husband was hiding, she got tangled in the web stretched over the doorway. She struggled and wriggled and managed to push her head through. And her husband, who had been outside all along, raised his axe and with a single blow – *wham!* – cut off her head.

Then he took to his heels and ran, with his wife's headless body in hot pursuit.

The head, meanwhile, had rolled out of the lodge and now it was bouncing along the ground after the children like a wayward rubber ball.

'Just you come back here! Stop when I'm talking to you. Bad, bad children!' And it rolled its eyes in fury and gnashed its teeth in rage.

But the children kept on running.

Now the head was gaining speed. It was getting closer. Quickly, one of the brothers took out the stick their father had given them and threw it over his shoulder. At once a dense thicket sprang up behind them. The head rolled straight into it and got snagged up in the twigs and branches. It pushed and pulled and struggled through the tangled growth until at last it was free. And then it was off again, rolling, tumbling, bouncing and bounding.

'Come back here at once, I say! Do what your mother tells you!'

But the children kept on running.

The head gained speed. It moved over the ground like a young hare, barely skimming the grass. Its eyes glinted malevolently; its mouth was stretched in a leer. Then the second brother took out the stone that their father had given them and threw it over his shoulder. At once a huge mountain sprang up behind them.

The head was unable to stop in time. It careered straight into the rock face, nose first. *Owww!* Then it rested where it had fallen, swaying gently from side to side and considering what to do next.

Just at that moment a column of ants came marching by, and the head persuaded them to dig a tunnel through the mountain, big enough to let it through. The ants got to work, and soon the head was on the other side, rolling, tumbling, bouncing and bounding along as before.

'Just wait till I catch up with you – then you'll see what happens to disobedient children!'

The head was coming on, faster and faster, closing the gap. In desperation, the first brother took out the last gift their father had given them – the handful of wet moss – and squeezed out the moisture it contained. At once a vast expanse of water spread out behind them. And the head, which was travelling at such a speed that it was unable to stop, fell into the water and drowned.

When the brothers saw that they were safe, they built themselves a raft and sailed back over the water to the land where they had come from. There they separated, each going his own way. One brother made the White Man. The other brother made the Blackfeet: that brother's name is Old Man Napi.

As for the body of their mother, it is still chasing their father. Round and round they go, in an eternal game of chase, for she is the Moon and he is the Sun. And as long as he can escape her, night will always follow day and day will always follow night.

Sky Spirit and Fine Weather Woman

NORTHWEST COAST

A CHIEF'S DAUGHTER WAS ONCE WALKING BY THE SEA when she heard the sound of a baby crying. She looked around. The beach seemed deserted, and yet the crying continued. At last, after much searching, she discovered that the sound was coming from inside a cockleshell. She lifted the shell, carefully prised it open and there, gurgling and chortling inside, was the most beautiful baby boy. He had a tuft of glossy black hair, shining black eyes and a dimpled smile.

The young woman took the baby home and brought him up as her own son. In time, she married and her husband, who was a skilled carpenter, built a fine wooden house for the three of them to live in, and so the little family began a happy life together.

While the chief's daughter attended to her daily work, she would keep her little son by her side and he would play contentedly, occupying himself in games of imagination, as children do. One day, she saw him pretending to shoot an invisible arrow from an invisible bow. 'He needs a real bow,' she thought, and so she took a copper bracelet and hammered it into shape and cut it, and made it into a miniature bow and a set of tiny arrows, which she gave to her child.

The little boy was delighted with his new toy and practised with it every day. In time, he became a skilled hunter and would bring back to his mother such small game as he had killed with his little bow and arrows – a rabbit perhaps, or a pigeon or two, and sometimes even a pheasant.

His parents were filled with pride at the precocious progress of their son: 'What a clever boy you are!' And in reply the child smiled his dimpled, rosy-cheeked smile.

'The boy certainly knows how to hunt, but what about fishing?' his father thought. So one day, when he was going out to fish, he decided to take his son with him. But, since the little lad was still small and was not ready to go out in a canoe on the ocean, he left the boy on the beach to watch him from there, and to learn by watching.

'Now you be a good boy and don't move till I get back,' the father told his son.

The boy did exactly as he was told. All the time his father was out in the canoe, he did not move from the spot but just sat silently watching the sea and the sky which, as if under the spell of his steady gaze, stayed calm and clement and blue so that his father was safe on the water.

Time passed and the boy grew in size and in strength until at last the day came when he was old enough to go out with his father in a canoe to the fishing ground. When they reached the place where the father wished to cast his line, his son whispered to him –

GOING FISHING

Both the Arctic and the Pacific Northwest – from which the legend of 'Sky Spirit and Fine Weather Woman' comes – had extensive coastlines and the tribes were therefore heavily dependent on the sea's bounty. The Indians of the Arctic took to the sea in a craft known as a *kayak*. Long and narrow like a canoe, this had a frame of driftwood reinforced with bone or ivory, and covered with waterproof, oiled sealskin. Closed in all around to keep out water, it had one cockpit, or sometimes two, into which the occupant could snugly tuck himself. Propelling his craft with a narrow wooden paddle, he was able to move over the water with great speed and agility in pursuit of seals and walruses. His weapons were a harpoon, a stabbing spear and a knife, and he also had a sealskin buoy to keep his catch afloat.

Whaling was another traditional activity among the Indians of the Arctic, and involved a larger craft called an *umiak*. With a driftwood frame covered with sealskin or walrus hide, powered by sails as well as paddles and up to 12 metres (40 feet) long, the *umiak* allowed whole crews to venture far out into the open sea in search of the massive bowhead whale.

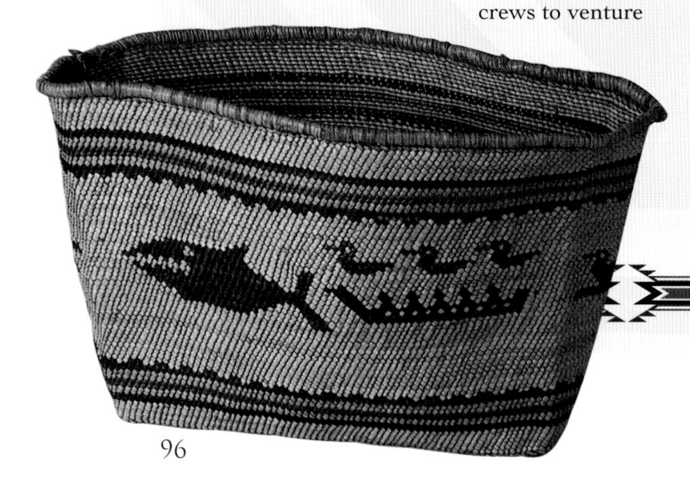

Whales were also hunted by Northwest Coast Indians. For the Nootka of Vancouver Island in particular, the hunt itself was elevated to the level of sacred ritual. The relationship between harpooner and quarry was a symbiotic one – the man had to 'be' the animal he would kill, showing that he could swim in deep, freezing waters, plunging and rolling like a whale. He also had to undergo a vision quest in search of a spirit guide.

His harpoon consisted of a yew-wood shaft up to 6 metres (20 feet) long, with a detachable elk-horn head tipped with razor-like mussel shell. When plunged into the animal's body, the head separated from the shaft and remained lodged in the body, while a cord of whale sinew, attached to the head and acting like a fishing line, kept the whale hooked. The men in the other canoes now approached and plunged in their harpoons, the final *coup de grâce* being administered by a chisel-headed lance.

The salmon was another important food source, and was indeed a dietary staple for the people of the Northwest Coast. Halibut was important, too. These were caught on beautifully made hooks of bent wood with bone tips, attached to lines made of kelp, an especially resilient seaweed.

'Repeat the words I say' – and no sooner were the words out of his father's mouth than the hook was seized and the line went taut and the canoe was dragged out to sea, at dizzying speed, by some invisible underwater force. Three times the boat was hauled around a little island that lay in the middle of the ocean, and the father could do nothing to prevent it. But when all was calm again and the father reeled in his line, there, on the end of it, was a fish of enormous size, brown and white with two shiny eyes on its right side – a halibut, and a magnificent catch.

After that, the boy always went fishing with his father, and as long as he was with him the father always had good luck.

The boy was growing into a handsome young man. And then a day came – his mother would never forget it – when he could not be found. His parents looked for him everywhere and called his name out loud. They searched the land. They searched the shore. They even searched the sea. He was nowhere to be seen.

Turning sadly homewards, they happened to look up into the sky ... and there, gliding over the ocean like some great sea bird with wings of cloud, was their son. He was dressed in a cloak of wren feathers, and the ocean beneath him was grey and cold.

When they looked up again the next day, there he was as before. But this time he wore a cloak of jay feathers, and the ocean beneath him was a sheet of silver and gold.

It was the same the next day, except that this time he was dressed in a cloak of woodpecker feathers, and the ocean beneath him glowed like fire.

It was then that his mother realized the truth, who the foundling really was whom she had discovered on the beach and had cared for all these years. He was none other than the Spirit of the Sky.

Sky Spirit came to visit his parents one last time. 'Do you remember,' he reminded his father, 'the day you first took me to watch you fish, when I was no more than a little child? And do you remember how I sat, looking at the sea and how, as long as I looked, the sea stayed calm? Well, it is still so. Look for my face in the sky and if you see it, gazing over the ocean, you will know it is safe to go fishing. And you, Mother,' he continued, 'you shall have a special place in the world in reward for all your years of devotion to me.'

And he handed his mother a cloak, a magic mantle. She put it on and she wears it still. When she sits by the ocean and opens it, all the winds and storms rush out. When she closes it, she draws them back inside. For she is Fine Weather Woman; wild or calm, the weather is hers to command. When her son grows angry and brooding and fills the sky with dark clouds, she takes a ball of white feathers and throws it up to him, to calm his temper. The feathers flutter back down to Earth. 'Look!' say the people, gazing up at the white-speckled heavens. 'Look,' they say, 'it is snowing!'

QUESTS AND SACRED GIFTS

SELU THE CORN MAIDEN

CHEROKEE/CREEK • SOUTHEAST

SELU, FIRST WOMAN, gave birth to twin boys. WAAAH! The babies yelled with hunger. That is how it started. And that is how it went on. These children were always hungry. 'Give us food, we want food,' they nagged when they were weaned and big enough to talk. 'There is nothing to eat!'

So Selu went out with her basket to find it. When she came back, her basket was full of kernels of corn. She ground the corn into a coarse meal, mixed the meal with water to make a paste, shaped the paste into rounds, and baked the rounds to make bread. The boys stuffed the hot bread into their greedy little mouths. It was good, very good, this freshly made bread.

Every day after that it was the same. Selu went out with her basket, filled it with corn, and baked the cornmeal rounds into bread. She was a loving, generous mother. Fed on this wholesome diet, her sons quickly grew in strength and size.

But as they grew, they ceased just to accept what they were given. They began to question. Where did their mother go every day? Where did she find the corn to make the bread of which they were so fond? They decided to follow her.

They saw her enter a log cabin. They peeped between a gap in the logs and watched. Their mother placed her basket on the ground and stood over it. Then she shook herself and – like blossoms drifting from the trees in spring or snowflakes floating from the winter sky – a shower of corn kernels cascaded from her body into the basket, filling it to the brim. So *that's* how she did it!

'We saw you, Mother,' the twins said to her later. 'We saw how you got the corn.'

Selu looked sad. 'Ah, so you know my secret? Now that you know it I must die.'

'No, no, that cannot be!'

'Yes, it must – and it is you yourselves who must kill me, and bury my body in the red earth. That is the way of it. But remember: out of my death something greater will come. Something to benefit all humankind. So when I am dead, do not grieve. Just remember me – and be grateful.'

Now her sons regretted their foolhardiness. Why had they given in to their curiosity?

But what was done was done. They could not go back. They could only do as Selu said.

And so it was that the twin brothers came to commit matricide, killing their own mother for the greater good of the human race. When they had killed her, they cut up her body, and buried it in the red earth just as she had told them to.

Winter came, and a hard time they had of it, for there was no Selu bearing home baskets of corn or baking bread. And then came spring, bringing a softness in the air and singing birds and a gentle sky. And out of the soil, in the places where Selu's body lay buried, little green sprouts pushed their way into the light. As spring gave way to summer, the sprouts became tall shoots and then strong stems with long leaves and fat cobs nestling between them. The dismembered body of Selu had become the first crop of maize.

The twin brothers harvested the maize and ground it into a coarse flour, and mixed the flour with water to make a paste, and shaped the paste into rounds, and baked the rounds to make bread, just as their mother had done before them. And it was good, very good, this freshly baked bread, and they ate it hungrily and were grateful.

But ever since that time, they – and the rest of the human race – have had to work, tilling and planting and harvesting, in order to provide their own food.

White Buffalo Woman and the Buffalo-Calf Pipe of Peace

SIOUX • PLAINS

Two hunters once went to find where the buffalo were. While they were out looking, they saw a figure far away in the distance, walking in their direction. They hid in some bushes and waited to see whether it was an enemy or friend.

The figure drew closer. It was not what they expected. It was a woman.

Over her arm the woman was carrying a bundle of sagebrush with something inside. And her face – ah, her face! It was beautiful, so beautiful.

'I have never seen such a beautiful woman,' said one of the men. 'I will make her my wife.'

'Have you gone mad?' hissed his companion. 'Look with the eyes in your head – can you not see what is perfectly plain? She is not one of us. She is a sacred being.' And so a whispered argument began between the two men. 'I will marry her! – No, you cannot, it would be sacrilege! How can you think such a thing? – 'I will do as I wish, and you cannot stop me!'

The woman looked straight in their direction. It was as if no distance existed between them, as if no bushes concealed them from view. Her gaze penetrated their hiding place as the sun's beams pierce the water.

'What is it that you wish?' she said, in a clear voice that sounded as if she were standing right next to them. 'Come, tell me what it is.'

The first man stepped boldly from the bushes, walked straight up to her and put his hands on her. 'I want you for my own.'

At once a whirlwind sprang up which stirred the grass and wrapped the pair in a shimmering vortex of dust and pollen and chaff. And then a mist, gossamer-fine,

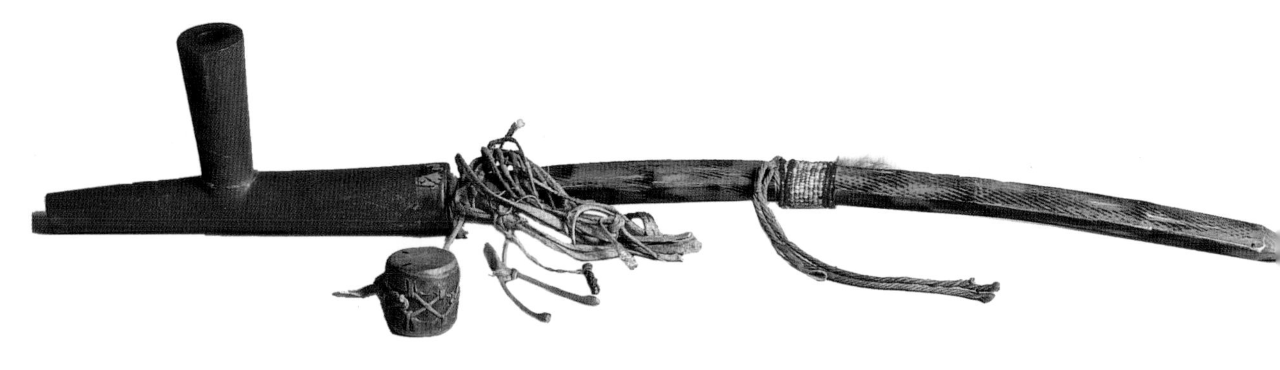

The White Buffalo

The white buffalo is especially revered by the Plains Indians. It is potent with sacred power, with divine, life-giving beneficence: it is 'big medicine'. The animal is extremely rare; according to traditional Lakota Sioux, only one white buffalo calf is born every four generations, appearing, like a saviour, in times of great trouble.

When a white buffalo was killed, both the arrow and the knife used to skin it were purified in burning sweetgrass smoke, and the hide was carefully removed so that none of the animal's blood could spill on it and mar its whiteness. The only men who could eat a white buffalo's flesh were those who had dreamed of animals. The only woman who could tan its hide was one known for her purity and goodness.

which shrouded them from all eyes.

When the mist cleared, the woman was still standing there, the sagebrush bundle on her arm.

But the man was no more than a bag of bones at her feet.

Silent with awe and wonder, his companion stood before the woman.

'I have come from the buffalo people,' she said. 'Go, and tell your people to prepare for me. This is what they must do: they must move camp and set up a new one, with their tipis arranged in a circle. They must leave an opening in the circle, and this opening must face north. In the middle of the circle they must set up a large tipi. This, too, must face north. When all this is ready I will come, to give my gift to the one among you called Bull Walking Upright.'

The man went running back to where his people were and passed on the message. All was done as the woman instructed.

Soon after, she arrived in the camp. She opened the sagebrush bundle she was carrying and inside was a red-stone pipe. A tiny buffalo calf was carved on its side. She gave the bundle to Bull Walking Upright. 'You are a good and worthy man,' she said. 'Here – take this pipe I give you, and keep it well for all the years of your life.'

And she told him when and how to use the pipe – when they prayed to Wakan Tanka, the Great Mysterious, whose being is in the blue of the sky and in the colours of the rainbow; when they prayed to the Earth, their mother. 'When you honour the Earth,' she said, 'you must dress as She does and as the buffalo do, in black and red and brown and white. Do these things for Wakan Tanka and for Mother Earth and

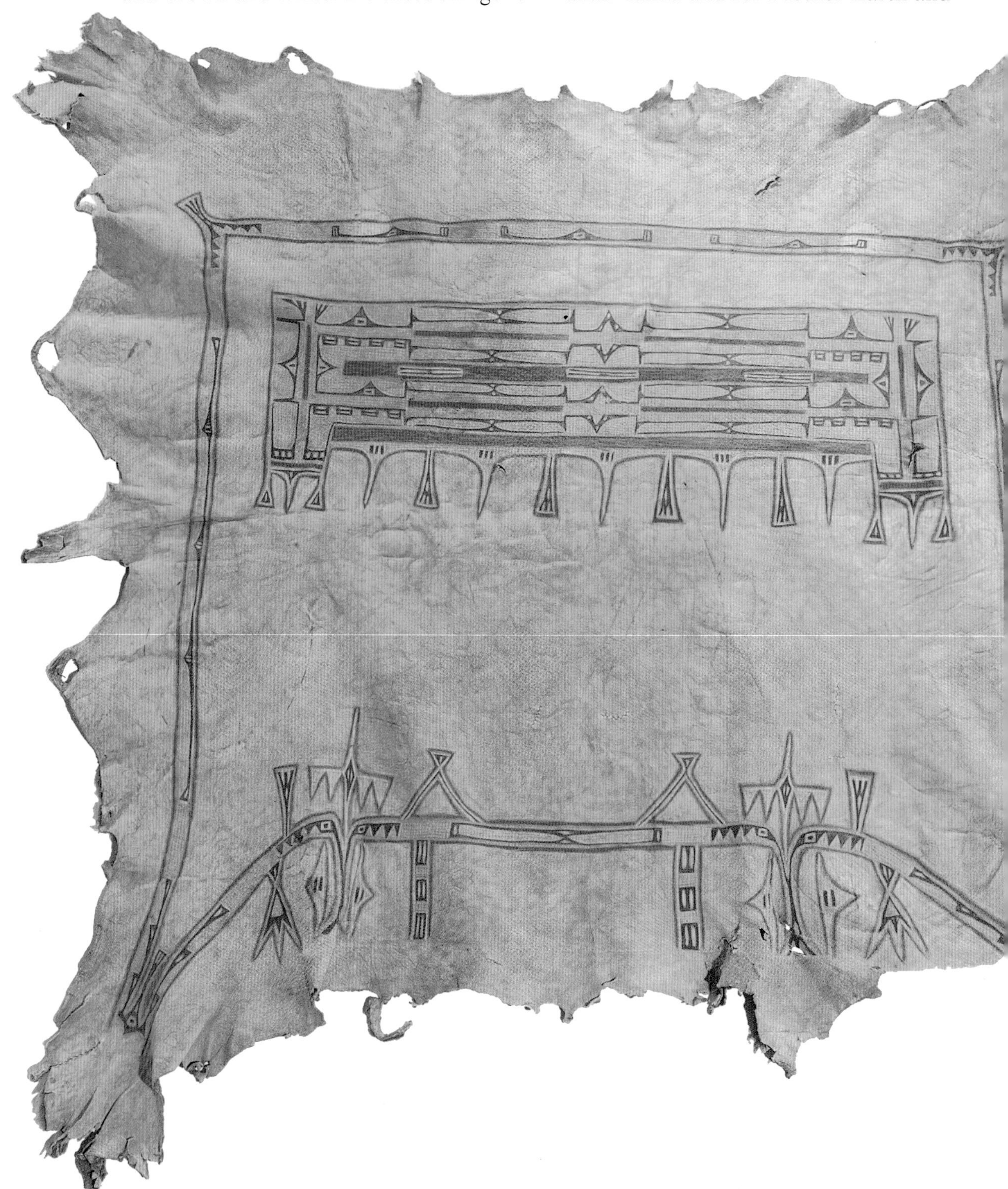

you will surely be blessed with all you ask for.'

And she taught Bull Walking Upright the prayers that should be said.

'Whenever you are hungry,' she continued, 'open the bundle and lay the pipe bare. Then the buffalo will know and they will come, and the hunters can kill them to feed all the people.'

'And, above all, remember ...' she concluded, 'that this is a pipe of peace. Smoke it before your ceremonies. Smoke it before making treaties. And it will fill your minds and your hearts with thoughts of peace. As long as you keep the pipe and use it, all will be well with your people.'

With these words, she turned on her heel and left, passing through the opening in the circle, walking northwards.

Just outside the circle, she lay down on the ground.

And when she got up, she was a black buffalo cow.

Walking northwards she went.

Then she lay down on the ground again.

And when she got up, she was a red buffalo cow.

Walking northwards she went.

Then she lay down on the ground again.

And when she got up, she was a brown buffalo cow.

Walking northwards she went.

Then she lay down on the ground again.

And when she got up, she was a white buffalo cow, as spotless as snow.

Walking northwards she went.

And vanished over the distant hills.

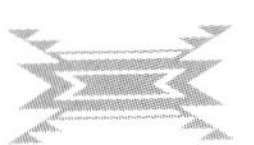

Bull Walking Upright kept the buffalo-calf pipe safely wrapped and used it as White Buffalo Woman had told him, bringing it out only for sacred ceremonies to which he had called all the people.

And when he was an old, old man, with long white hair and twinkling, crinkled eyes and rich in the wisdom of years, he passed on the pipe and the knowledge he had been given to his successor, a man called Sunrise. And so the buffalo-calf pipe and the knowledge of how to use it was passed on down from one generation to the next ...

As long as you keep the pipe and use it, all will be well with your people.

Bith Ahatini and the Night Chant

NAVAJO • SOUTHWEST

There were once three brothers. The eldest was rich, the youngest was a growing boy, and the middle brother – well, he was a wayward fellow who liked to gamble and tell tall tales of all he had done and seen in his rovings out in the wide, wide world. Because of this, his brothers had a special name for him: they called him Bith Ahatini, the Dreamer.

One day, the eldest brother and the youngest brother decided to go hunting. They asked their sister's husband to go with them. But they did not ask Bith Ahatini. 'Let us go without him lest he steal what is ours and gamble it away.' And so, in the cool dawn, the three men crept silently and secretly away from the village.

It was four days before the Bith Ahatini, in his dreamy way, realized that he had been duped. But, never daunted, he decided to follow them. 'Perhaps they will let me carry their game – and give me a pelt or two for my trouble,' he thought.

And so he set off.

Up hill and down hill he went, across valley and creek.

But he did not find them.

At last, as the Sun was descending to his home in the west and coating the land with gold, Bith Ahatini came to a deep, rocky canyon. From its shadowy depths he heard harsh voices calling. He stepped up to the edge and peered down. Crows! Hundreds of crows were wheeling and swooping in an aerial dance, their coal-black wings spread out, buoyed on the rising air. *Croak, croak,* they cried as they disappeared into openings in the canyon walls. *Caw, caw.*

As night fell, the sound of other voices floated up from the canyon. This time Bith Ahatini found that he could understand what they said.

'It is a sad day indeed, my brother. Yes, a very sad day,' bemoaned one.

'Why? What happened today?' asked the other.

'Did you not hear the news? Two men died this day – shot by hunters with arrows while they were out looking for food!'

'Hunters! Have we not always said: be on your guard against hunters?'

'Yes, yes, we have, many a time. But the two who died were not on their guard – and now it is too late. Aah, the sorrow and the pity of it!'

This was indeed strange. Who did the voices belong to? Despite the darkness of the night and the shiver of fear that shot through him, Bith Ahatini peered down into the

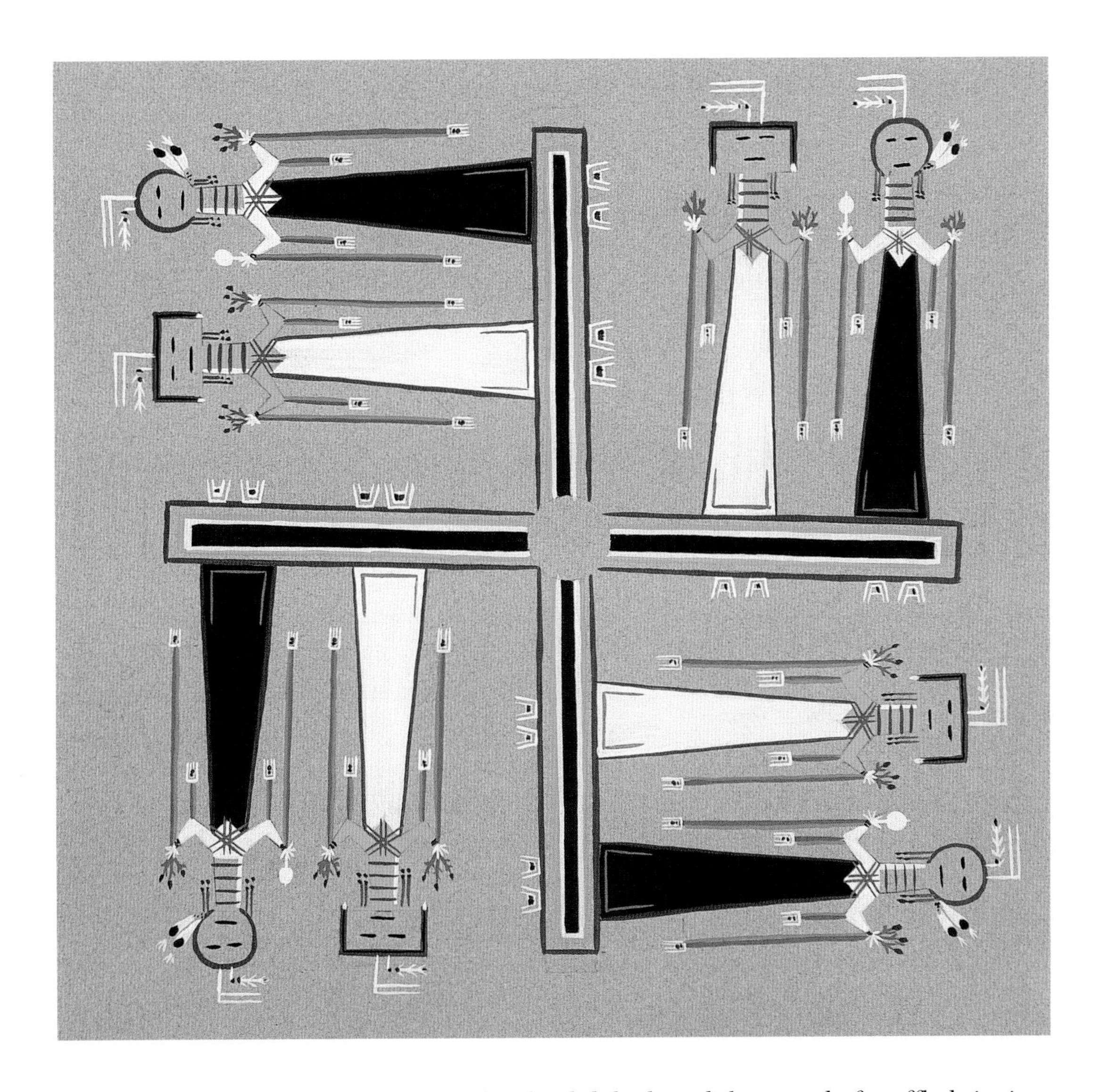

canyon to see what he might see. And as he did, he heard the sound of muffled singing, and saw, in the openings of the canyon walls, a hundred fires lighting a hundred dancers. *Thrum, thrum* went their feet as they stamped out the rhythm of the dance. *Chik-chika-chik* went their rattles, keeping time.

He realized that he was in the presence of sacred beings – animal spirits who were both Bird and Man.

The dancing and chanting went on all night. But, as day dawned, the dancers disappeared.

Bith Ahatini resumed his search for his brothers. 'Wait till I find them and tell them what I have seen!' he thought. 'They will never believe it!'

And he was right – they didn't. 'You spent the night by a sacred canyon? And heard crows speaking with the voices of men?' said his older brother, laughing. 'What will you think of next?'

'And the crows turned into people ...' cried his younger brother, holding his sides, 'and danced a sacred dance with drums and rattles?'

'And when day came, they were gone?' said his sister's husband. 'Please tell me more.'

And while Bith Ahatini's brothers packed up to go home, he told his brother-in-law

THE NIGHT CHANT

The nine-day Night Chant, or Night Way, which Bith Ahatini – literally 'His-Visions' but usually translated as 'The Visionary' or 'The Dreamer' – brought to the Navajo was one of many 'Chants' or 'Ways' which formed part of a whole system of sacred ceremonies. Usually conducted as healing rituals, either for individuals or for the benefit of the community, these included Blessing Way, Beauty Way, Mountain Way and many others, each with its own functions, songs and associated myths.

The *hataali*, or singer – the shamanic figure who conducted the Chants – had to know the entire complex sequence of each ritual by heart, and had to be word-perfect in his recitation of hundreds of songs. On the ninth night of the Night Chant, for example, the singing – according to Washington Matthews writing in 1902 in 'The Night Chant, a Navaho Ceremony' (*Memoirs of the American Museum of Natural History*) – continued uninterrupted 'from dark until daylight'. Because of these demands on memory, singers tended to specialize in a limited number of ceremonies.

Another distinctive feature of the Chants was the ceremonial sand altars or sand paintings depicting mythological and sacred images. These 'dry-paintings' were created on the floor of the hogan, or dwelling, by the hataali, using coloured sands, pollens, cornmeal, crushed dried flowers, charcoal and sandstone. Taking several hours to complete, they were so beautiful and so powerful in their depiction of the spirits that they drew those spirits to them, thus acting as a conduit between the human participants and the supernatural. When the ceremony was over, the sand paintings were destroyed. Modern sand paintings produced for commercial reasons contain deliberate mistakes in order not to offend the spirits.

the whole story of what he had seen and heard. He told him, too, about the men who had died. 'You were the hunters who shot them,' he said.

'Oh, no, no, that cannot be,' replied his brother-in-law. 'We killed a crow and a magpie, certainly. But we killed no men.'

'But they *were* men, out hunting for food like you – they had only taken on the shapes of birds.' And his brother-in-law saw the truth of his words, and was greatly sorry for what they had done.

When the pair caught up with the two brothers who had gone ahead, they found themselves by the side of the same canyon where Bith Ahatini had seen the Bird People. As they stood there, looking down, four mountain sheep came towards them, picking their way between the rocks and boulders. The two brothers and their brother-in-law quickly dropped out of sight while Bith Ahatini ran on ahead, hid, and waited.

As the sheep drew near, he raised his bow to shoot the one in the lead. But his arrow would not leave the bowstring. He ran on ahead and tried again. Again the arrow would not move. He tried twice more. Each time the same thing happened. He looked at the sheep again. But they were no longer there. In their place were four spirit beings, wearing masks.

'Come with us,' said the first of them, 'we are going to perform a sacred ceremony, a Chant, four days' journey from here.'

'Oh, but I could not – for you are spirits and I ... well, I am only a man.'

'I will make you as we are. Remove your clothes.'

And so, Bith Ahatini, at last persuaded, took off his clothes, and the spirit breathed over him and blew away his humanness. Then the five took four steps to the east, changed into mountain sheep, and trotted off along the path.

Meanwhile, in their hiding place, the brothers were still waiting.

'Where is he? Why is he taking so long? What is he up to now?' the eldest brother grumbled. But when they went to look for Bith Ahatini, and found his clothes, and traced his footsteps and saw where they turned into hoofprints alongside those of the four sheep, the brothers realized that his tale of animal spirits had been true all along. 'Forgive me, forgive me,' said the elder one, weeping. But his tears met with silence, for the one he cried out to was gone.

Up hill and down hill, across valley and creek went Bith Ahatini and his spirit companions.

At last they came to a large hogan, an earth lodge. Inside a big crowd was gathered. 'What is that scent – that smell?' they cried out in disgust as Bith Ahatini entered. 'That stench of *human* flesh?' The beings who had brought him took him outside and washed him with yucca-root to remove the offending odour.

Back inside the hogan Bith Ahatini looked around. There were four posts on which the spirits' masks were hanging, for those gathered there were animal-people just like the crows and the sheep. The posts were placed according to the four directions. The eastern one was made of white shell, the southern one of turquoise, the western one of abalone, the northern one of jet.

On the west side of the hogan lay two pipes. Filling them with tobacco and lighting them, the animal spirit nearest them passed them to his neighbours on either side. The whole company smoked in turn, the last to do so being the two owl spirits who sat on either side of the entrance. Drawing deeply on the pipes, all took in the smoke and puffed it out, sending spirals of the sweetly scented vapour floating up, heavenwards. Water Sprinkler – who had initially been forgotten and had shown his anger at this sleight by releasing a violent storm – joined in, too, and was placated and soothed by the sacred smoke.

And then the Chant began. On the floor of the hogan, the animal spirits unfolded white deerskins on which sacred pictures had been painted. And so beautiful and so holy were these pictures that the gods themselves came to look, to see their image in them and to hear the prayer that was sung, slow and steady, rhythmic and hypnotic …

O male divinity
With your moccasins of dark cloud,
come to us
With your mind enveloped in dark cloud,
come to us
With the dark thunder above you,
come to us soaring
With the shapen cloud at your feet,
come to us soaring …

All that day and for eight days more the Chant continued,
with new painted deerskins unrolled as the ceremony progressed …

My feet restore for me
My limbs restore, my body restore, my mind restore,
my voice restore for me …

And the beauty of the paintings and the power in the smoke and in the Chant and in the rhythm of the dance called down healing and blessings and happiness. And made all the gods smile.

Bith Ahatini was allowed home just long enough to teach the ceremony to his younger brother – to teach him *Kieje Hatal*, the Night Chant, so that he could teach it to the *De'ne*, the People, the Navajo Indians. And when Bith Ahatini had done what he had gone to do, he left his people and went to live among the gods forever.

On the trail marked with pollen I walk
With grasshoppers about my feet I walk
With dew about my feet I walk
With beauty I walk
With beauty before me I walk
With beauty behind me I walk
With beauty above me I walk
With beauty about me I walk
It is finished in beauty
It is finished in beauty

Tiyo and the Snake Dance

HOPI • SOUTHWEST

The great Colorado River cuts its way through the landscape, gouging out a path through the rock. It has been doing this for millennia, relentlessly, untiringly, eating away at the body of the Earth and opening a fissure in her side which is now a canyon so wide and so deep that its floor is lost in shadow. The walls of the canyon glow in the sunset, revealing the red and brown layers of rock where the Earth's flesh has been cut away.

Tiyo, a son of a great chief, liked to sit on the rim of the canyon, and dream. Down there, he could see the great river, moving purposefully along. Where did it come from? Where did it go?

'I am going,' he told his father, 'to find where the river ends.' And, since he was a young man and of an age to undertake such quests, his father gave him his blessing, for who knows what wisdom may be gained, when a man goes out into the world to seek what will come?

Everything was made ready for his journey. Tiyo and his friends built a boat which could be closed over on all sides so that the occupant within was kept safe and dry, like a pupa snug in its cocoon. He made a pole, too, to push and steer the boat through the water. The shaman – the priest – tied prayer sticks to the top of the pole, and sang prayers of blessing.

And then it was time to leave. Tiyo's father and his warriors piled his boat, waiting in the shallows, with food and prayer sticks tipped with feathers. 'May the spirits protect you, my son,' said his father, as he bid him goodbye.

Picking up his pole, Tiyo pushed off from the bank and moved into the deeper water, and the current took hold of the boat and carried it away.

As he drifted along, Tiyo gazed about him in wonder. The walls of the canyon towered above him on either side. High up, aspens, firs and spruce spread their branches against a turquoise sky. Lower down, junipers and pines scented the air. The canyon was a whole world to itself, teeming with life. Pronghorns and bighorn sheep picked their way along the flats and ledges, nibbling at herbs and leaves. Lizards scuttled, snakes coiled, squirrels leapt, beavers swam, and mountain lions slept, waiting for night – the time of the hunt – to fall.

Tiyo ate the food he had been given and caught fish from the river, and drank from it too. It tasted fresh and clean. And all the while, the river carried him along on its strong, broad back. Sometimes it was calm and peaceful; at other times, it raged, working itself into a foaming fury as it hurled itself over the rock falls in its course. But, with the aid of his pole and the shaman's magic, Tiyo survived all these hazards.

Then, slowly, the landscape began to change – it was broader, flatter. The river was growing broader too, opening out, its banks shrinking away until Tiyo could hardly see them any more. He and his boat were no more than a tiny speck in the middle of a shimmering sheet of water which seemed to have neither beginning nor end.

He had achieved his goal.

He had reached the river's end.

He had reached the Big Water, where the Sun goes to sleep at night.

Far away, out on the water, Tiyo saw an island. Using his pole like an oar, he paddled towards it. He landed on the shore.

Before him stood a house. But the entrance to it was so small that he could not enter. 'Come in, come in,' said a voice from inside and – magically – the entrance stretched to allow him through.

Inside the house sat Spider Woman. 'Welcome, my son.' Tiyo presented her with one of the prayer sticks he had been given, as a gift.

'I have come,' he said, 'seeking the end of the great river. And now that I have found it, I must return to my people. But I wish to take something with me – a token, a sign, a present – in gratitude to them, and to show them that I reached my journey's end.'

'Ah!' said Grandmother Spider. 'I know where you can find just such a thing. Not far from here is a house of treasures where you may find many gemstones and beautiful beads. These you could take to your people. But beware, for the way there is fraught with dangers – wild beasts who would tear your flesh and crush your bones and poison your blood and swallow you in a single gulp. Here – take this and it will protect you.' Spider Woman gave Tiyo a small jar filled with a magical liquid. 'And so that you can find your way, I will come with you.' And she hopped onto Tiyo's neck and, tucking in all her eight little legs, curled up behind his ear, where she could whisper directions and words of encouragement to him

Before Tiyo had got very far, he came to a patch of marshy ground. He could not get across. If he dared to place his foot on it, he would be sucked helplessly down, that was perfectly plain. 'The lotion!' hissed Spider

Woman from behind his ear. 'Use the lotion!'

So Tiyo sprinkled a few drops on the ground and at once a rainbow appeared before him – a rainbow bridge on which he was able to cross the marsh.

But he was not out of danger yet. Hardly had he set foot on firm ground again when, with a terrible roar, an enormous puma lunged at him, claws out, fangs bared. 'The lotion, the lotion!' yelled Spider Woman. Tiyo sprinkled the puma with it, and the beast at once recoiled and lay down, as docile as a kitten, to lick its fur.

Next came a bear, then a wildcat, then a wolf, then a rattlesnake. But, by using the magic lotion, Tiyo calmed them all in the same way.

At last he reached the house of treasures. A ladder led up to an entrance in the roof, from which another ladder led down into the interior. Tiyo climbed up, then down, with Spider Woman still hiding behind his ear.

The inside of the house was large, with a fire in the middle. Snakeskins hung from the ceiling and walls, and warriors were sitting in a circle that ran all around the room. Their faces were painted and they wore bright beads around their necks. All were silent and sat gazing intently at Tiyo, who had taken up a place by the fire.

The silence continued. Then the chief of the company picked up his pipe and lit it. He drew on it four times. He handed the pipe to Tiyo and watched, to see what he would do. Tiyo also smoked it four times. 'Ah, ha-ha! It is good! Welcome, welcome!' And the chief and his warriors greeted the newcomer warmly, like a brother. Tiyo, in return, gave them each a feather-tipped prayer stick.

'Now it is time to put on our snakeskins,' said the chief.

Tiyo was asked to turn away while they did this. When he turned back, he was no longer in a room with men like him but in a serpent's den with snakes writhing all over the floor. Black snakes, brown snakes, red snakes, striped and spotted and patched snakes, snakes as thin as a reed and as fat as a trunk, snakes with muscles to squeeze the breath out of a man, snakes with darting tongues and venom-filled fangs for killing.

'Don't be afraid,' said a voice in Tiyo's ear. 'I am here. I will tell you what to do.'

Great Snake, the chief, who was now a magnificent rattlesnake with black bands across his golden body and golden rattles tipping his tail, reared up before him. 'If you can choose which one of us is my daughter,' he said, 'we will let you into all our secrets.'

'The yellow rattler! She's the yellow rattler!' hissed the voice behind his ear again, too faint for anyone but Tiyo to hear.

'Hmm, a most difficult choice. Shall it be – the thin black one over there? Or what about the stripy red one over here? No, no ... wait ... now let me think. Yes, I think she must be ... this yellow rattlesnake, right here in front of me!' And as Tiyo spoke these words, the snake's skin fell away and before him stood the most beautiful young woman

THE SNAKE DANCE

The Snake Dance, said to have been brought to the Hopi Indians by their hero Tiyo, was one of the most important Hopi sacred ceremonies. Its purpose was to bring rain: in Hopi belief, snakes were seen as 'elder brothers' and were thought to have power over the rainmaking spirits.

Organized and performed by initiates of the Snake and Antelope societies, the ritual – which was largely secret – required two weeks of preparation. Snakes were gathered from the four cardinal directions, made 'brothers' of the Snake society, ritually washed and placed in a special snake house or *kisi*. A sand altar, like those made by the Navajo (see 'The Night Chant', page 108), was also prepared for use during the ceremony.

The Dance itself was performed in public. Holding wooden prayer sticks painted to represent snakes and wearing tortoiseshell or deer-hoof rattles on their knees to imitate the sound of a rattlesnake, the participants formed a line and began a low chant. As their chanting increased in volume, they moved in an undulating wave towards the kisi. Here, each dancer was given a live rattlesnake which he would continue to hold in his mouth while he circled the village square four times. When all the snakes had been exhibited in this way, the Dance finished. The reptiles were then returned to the desert and set free in sacred places at the four points of the compass, bearing the Hopi prayers for rain – animal intermediaries between man and the spirits of nature.

Public performances of the spectacular Hopi Snake Dance have been continued up to the present day, and attract vast crowds.

he had ever set eyes on.

And so it was, because he had made the right choice, that Tiyo was initiated into the sacred mysteries of the Snake Dance.

The Snake People showed him how they put on their snakeskins.

They sang for him the words of praise and thanks, so that he might learn them.

They danced the dance for him so that he could learn the steps.

They showed him their sand altar.

When Tiyo had learned all these things, he thanked the Snake People and returned with Spider Woman to her house by the way that they had come. Here, he gave her another prayer stick in thanks. She, in her turn, gave him a treasure from each of the four rooms of her house. From her east room, she gave him a white shell; from her south room, a red bead; from her west room, a large turquoise; from her north room, a small turquoise.

The following day, Tiyo returned to the Snake People to say goodbye. 'Farewell, my son,' said the chief. 'You came alone, but you will not return alone. Here is your bride. My blessing on you both.' And Snake Maiden, the chief's daughter, stepped up to Tiyo, with a shy smile on her face.

Tiyo and his new wife returned to his own country, by land, following the course of the Colorado River. He was welcomed home like a hero, and his wife was warmly greeted, too.

Tiyo told his people all that he had seen on his quest.

He told them about the canyon and all the birds and animals and trees there.

He told them about Spider Woman and how she had helped him.

He gave them the gemstones he had brought.

And he taught them the Snake Dance, which he had learned from the Snake People who live on an island in the Big Water where the Sun goes to sleep at night.

Ever since then, the people have danced the Snake Dance, with snakes taken from the four directions – east, south, west and north – as a prayer to the gods to send rain.

POIA AND THE SUN DANCE

BLACKFEET • PLAINS

EARLY ONE MORNING, before the Sun had risen, when trails of mist still hung over the meadows and the birds were only beginning to stir, Feather Woman awoke outside the lodge where she had been sleeping. She yawned and stretched and looked up at the dawn sky. And there, in the slowly lightening expanse of turquoise blue, she saw the Morning Star. He was so bright and so beautiful that he took her breath away. It was at that moment that she fell in love. 'I will have no one else for my husband but the Star of the Morning,' she thought.

Every day after that she would get up early in time to see her beloved, before his brilliance was eclipsed by the rising Sun.

Up in the sky, Morning Star saw her, too – saw her devotion and her love, and his heart softened. 'I will have no one else for my wife but Feather Woman,' he thought.

And so it was, one day, as she was walking by the riverside, that Feather Woman came face to face with Morning Star, who had come down from the sky to see her. 'Be

my bride,' he said, 'and live with me in heaven.' And he took a yellow feather from his headdress and gave it to her to hold in one hand, and a juniper spray in the other. He told her to shut her eyes, and when she opened them again she was standing by his side in the Sky-country, in the land of the Sun and the Moon.

Eight, nine, ten months went by and Feather Woman gave birth to a baby boy. He was named Little Star. As a gift to the new mother, the Moon, Morning Star's mother and wife of the Sun, his father, gave her a root digger.

'This will make your daily work easier,' she said. 'Use it to dig up any edible roots that you find except for one – the turnip that grows by the house of Spider Man. Remove that and the greatest sorrow will follow.'

But a warning given is a snare laid, and curiosity about the forbidden root gnawed at Feather Woman's imagination. What was so special about this particular vegetable? What made it different from all the others? What harm could possibly come of digging it up? She decided to take a little look ... not to remove the turnip from the soil, you understand, but just to examine it in the place where it grew.

And so in the end, Feather Woman did exactly what the Moon said she should not do – she went secretly to the house of the Spider Man and began to scrape carefully away at the soil with her digger. And there was the turnip! She could just see the top. She continued scraping. The soil was fine and crumbly and fell away like sand, and before she had time to realize what had happened, the turnip was free and lying, plump and long and white, on the ground before her. And where it had been in the soil, there was now a hole which, by some curious magic, seemed to be getting bigger by the minute. It was a cavity – no, a chasm – through which she could see all of the Earth, laid out like a blanket of greens and yellows and blues, far, far below.

Now Feather Woman understood. Now she knew why the Moon had warned her. The turnip was the plug that stopped the hole in heaven – and she had removed it!

But what was done could not be undone and Feather Woman looked down through the opening she had made in the sky, at the world beneath. There were the prairies and the herds of buffalo that she remembered so well; there was the river where her people used to fish; there were their tipis with the smoke rising through the smoke-holes at the top. And when she saw all these things, her heart was filled with such homesickness that it almost burst.

But worse was yet to come.

When the Moon discovered Feather Woman's disobedience, she told her husband the Sun, and the Sun was angry and turned the young woman and her son out of heaven, lowering them to Earth on a silken thread spun by the Spider Man. Down, down, down through the dark night sky floated Feather Woman, clutching her child to her. Glancing up from below, those who saw stared in wonder. 'Look!' they cried. 'A falling star!'

Mother and son landed on the edge of the camp, and Feather Woman went at once to find her parents who had never known why their daughter had disappeared, never known that she had married a god. 'We thought we had lost you for ever!' they cried. 'We thought you were dead!' With tears in their eyes, they welcomed their daughter and grandson, and Feather Woman told them everything that had happened to her, and how now she was exiled from heaven.

But worse was yet to come.

Although it was good to be with her own kind once more, doing all the things that she used to do, Feather Woman knew that she was parted from her husband forever. She could see him up in the sky, looking sadly down at her, but the space between them was as wide as eternity and as unbridgeable. If only she could turn back time, if only she could undo what she had done ... 'if only' – the two saddest words ever uttered by the human tongue. And so burdened was Feather Woman by her grief and her sense of loss that in the end her heart burst and she died, leaving her son an orphan.

Little Star continued to live among the Blackfeet, his mother's people, but in the deepest poverty for by now his grandparents, too, were dead and he was all alone in the world.

Orphaned, he grew to manhood, and he was a fine enough young man except for one thing: his face was marked by a scar so that some of the people mocked him and gave him a cruel name, as ignorant folk often will. They nicknamed him *Poia*, which means 'Scar Face'.

Now there was in the camp a beautiful young woman, the daughter of a chief, and Poia fell in love with her. But seeing only his exterior disfigurement and not his good, inner heart, she laughed when he proposed to her. 'I cannot marry a man with a scar! Get rid of the scar and then – maybe, just maybe – I will think about marrying you.'

Hanging his head in shame and sorrow, Poia went to consult a medicine woman. 'How can I get rid of this scar?' he asked.

THE SUN DANCE

For several nomadic Plains Indians tribes, the Sun Dance was the most important sacred rite of the year. It was traditionally held at midsummer when the Sun is at its zenith in the sky. The event took place in and around a ceremonial lodge which symbolized the universe. Similarly, the pole at its centre – a tree which had been specially cut, trimmed, painted and decorated – represented the World Tree or *axis mundi*, the axis of the universe.

During the course of a day, the dancers would move around the periphery of the lodge, gazing at the Sun as continuously as possible – the name 'Sun Dance' may come from the Sioux who refer to part of the ceremony as 'sun gazing'.

The Sun Dance also included an act of self-sacrifice in which certain participants would allow themselves to be suspended from the central pole by means of skewers inserted into their breasts or backs. Encouraged by the singing and drumming of the spectators, they would remain suspended while praying to the Sun for guidance and blowing on an eagle-bone whistle. Although this practice must have seemed barbaric to early white observers, it does have parallels in European myth and mystery. Odin, Norse father god and world magician, indulged in a similar act of shamanic self-sacrifice when he hung for nine days and nights on Yggdrasil, the World Tree that supports the Norse universe. His prize, at the end of his trial, was the discovery of the Runes, the Nordic divinatory system. Likewise, the Hanged Man card of the Tarot achieves enlightenment through patient ordeal.

Bound to the Sun in mystical union, the participants were now prepared for the great midsummer hunts to come. The Sun Dance of the nomadic tribes of the Plains is similar to parts of the *O-kee-pa* ceremony of the Mandan, a Plains tribe who lived in semi-permanent earth-lodge villages.

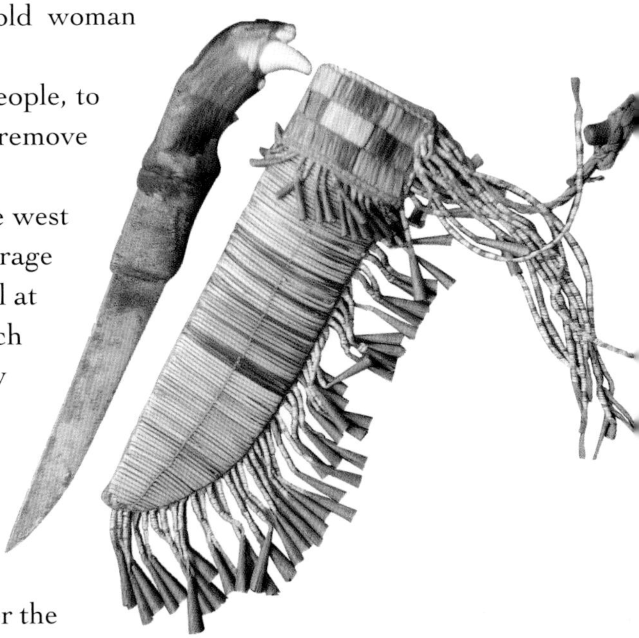

'You have been marked by the Sun,' the old woman replied. 'Only the Sun can undo his own mark.'

And so Poia left the camp, left his mother's people, to seek his grandfather the Sun and to ask him to remove his scar.

It was a long, long road he had to walk, to the west where the Sun goes to bed at night, but with courage in his heart he began, journeying westward, until at last he reached the ocean, the Big Water, which stretched before him as vast as infinity. How would he ever get across?

Trusting to his fate, Poia stopped and spent three days by the shore, fasting and praying. And when he awoke on the morning of the fourth day, he saw a wide and shining golden path stretching as far as he could see, over the water. He stepped onto the path which bore his weight without sinking, and he walked and he walked and he walked all the way across the Big Water to the home of his grandfather, the Sun.

Poia bided his time, waiting for the right moment to approach the Sun, and it was then that he caught sight of his father, Morning Star. He was trying to fight off seven ferocious birds who were attacking him, and it looked as if he was getting the worst of it. Blood streaked his face and his arms where the birds' beaks and talons had broken his skin, and his brilliance was waning, like a fading flame. Drawing on all the warrior's skill that he had learned from his mother's people, Poia rushed upon the monsters and, slashing to the right and left, killed them all, thus saving his father's life.

News of this brave act was soon made known to the Sun and Poia was called before him. He stood humbly before his grandfather, a poor and ragged wanderer with an ugly scar across his face, but his grandfather knew him for who he was.

'Child of my own blood, welcome!' said the Sun.

'Son of my own blood, thank you,' said Morning Star.

And in a spirit of reconciliation and as a reward for his bravery, the Sun gave Poia three gifts.

As his first gift, the Sun lightly brushed his grandson's cheek with his shining hand. 'Be whole!' he said. And when Poia felt his face, the scar was gone and the skin there was as velvet-smooth as the hide of a newborn buffalo calf. He was no longer Poia, 'Scarface': he was Little Star.

As his second gift, the Sun placed two raven's feathers in his grandson's hair as a sign of acceptance and kinship.

As his third gift, the Sun gave his grandson a pipe whose sweet and magical music would win for him the heart of the proud chief's daughter.

The Sun also taught him the secrets of the Sun Dance, and told him to take this knowledge to the Blackfeet people.

Armed with all these gifts, Little Star returned to Earth by way of the Wolf Trail – the silver trail of stars that white men call the Milky Way. And when the proud chief's daughter saw Little Star without a blemish on his face, and when she heard him play on his magic pipe music of such beauty and enchantment, she fell in love with him on the spot. The pair were married and Little Star took his bride up to his grandfather's home in the sky, just as his father had done before him, and there they are still to this day, walking for ever arm in arm and step by step across the flower-starred prairie of heaven.

MONDAWMIN THE CORN SPIRIT

CHIPPEWA/OJIBWA • NORTHEAST

IN THE FAR-OFF LONG AGO, there lived a man and wife and their children. To provide food for his family, the father would go out hunting, and his wife and those children who were old enough would gather berries and fruits from the bushes. In this way they sustained their lives, dependent on the bounty of the Earth. But when winter came and the snow fell, covering the land in a fleecy blanket of whiteness, and the water in the lakes froze to milky ice, there was often no food to be had and then the man and his family would go hungry.

Now the man's eldest son was approaching the age when he would undertake his spirit quest to meet his spirit guardian who would be his guide through life, and to be given his spirit name. This quest was something that he must do alone, in a place apart from all human habitation. And so Eldest Son prepared a solitary hut, and settled down to begin his seven-day fast and to await whatever visions and visitations should come.

On the first day of his fast, Eldest Son got up and went for a walk in the forest. The air was scented with the sweet smell of fallen leaves and in the shafts of sunlight which filtered through the trees, clouds of tiny insects billowed. As he made his way between oaks and

THE VISION QUEST

Although the shaman achieved the highest level of interaction with the spirit world, that did not prohibit ordinary members of the population from communing with the spirits, who were viewed as a source of power and protection. While the Indians of some regions allowed the spirits to come to them spontaneously in dreams, others sought them actively by means of a Vision Quest, as described in 'Mondawmin the Corn Spirit'.

The Vision Quest was often an initiatory rite, undertaken by young men and sometimes women at puberty; it might also be required at times of difficulty in other periods of life. It generally involved seclusion from the rest of the community, and fasting to achieve the state of altered consciousness necessary to open the mind to another reality. Among Plateau tribes, for example, all boys and some girls were sent off on a solitary vigil in which they hoped to meet their spirit guide. On their return, they did not speak of the experience until adulthood, which could be as much as ten years later. Only at death might a man reveal his spirit song, which others would then sing to him.

On the Plains as in the Plateau region, the seeker was usually a youth for whom the Vision Quest was a rite of passage into manhood. Under the guidance of a shaman, he prepared for his vigil with several days of purification, after which he retired to a remote and often sacred spot, such as a mountaintop, where he fasted and prayed, and waited for visions to come. On his return, the shaman interpreted his experience and gave him his sacred song and his personal magical charm, which might be a shell, a feather, or a claw, for example. Later, the young man would carry this object with him into battle as a source of supernatural help. Although it was important for Plains Indians to acquire at least one spirit helper to guide them through life, the Vision Quest did not always reveal one. Hunger, lack of sleep, and the cold in the remote places chosen for such vigils sometimes led to failure. The ritual would then be repeated at another time.

In the Northeast, Menominee boys and girls underwent a similar rite at puberty, known as the Great Fast. Blackening their faces, they secluded themselves in the woods and remained there, alone, without food for as long as ten days. Visitations by Upper World spirits such as White Bear or Golden Eagle denoted a successful quest; Horned Snake or other Lower World beings indicated failure. The initiate was allowed four attempts at a Vision Quest. If desirable spirits still did not appear, he or she was doomed to life as a witch.

maples, he glimpsed a deer in a thicket just ahead of him, and a rabbit which hopped across his path. He looked up at the fretwork of branches above him. He saw the squirrel with his hoard of nuts, the pigeon by her nesting place, and higher even than that, in the little patches of sky which stretched between the branches like scraps of blue cloth, he caught sight of the wild goose, flying across the forest canopy towards the lake.

All this bounty was the Great Spirit's doing, and Eldest Son was grateful. But he remembered the forest in winter and how, in that lifeless season, a man might starve for want of game. If only there was an easier way to find food! And he raised his thoughts in silent prayer.

'Master of Life, help my people.'

On the second day of his fast, Eldest Son went for a walk in the meadow that lay between the forest and the river. The flower-starred grass waved in the wind and the warm air hummed with the droning of bees. Fruit hung in swollen bunches from the blackcurrant and blueberry bushes, and beneath them the wild strawberry spread its carpet of red and green. Near to the river where the reeds grew, the wild rice rose in fertile clumps out of the boggy soil.

All this bounty was the Great Spirit's doing, and Eldest Son was grateful. But he remembered the meadow in winter and how, in that lifeless season, a man might starve for want of berries and seeds. If only there was an easier way to find food! And he raised his thoughts in silent prayer.

'Master of Life, help my people.'

On the third day of his fast, Eldest Son went for a walk by the lake. The water was still and reflected the sky like a giant's mirror. With flashes of silver fin and tail, the trout, sturgeon and bass swam by, while in the shallows the pike lay waiting.

All this bounty was the Great Spirit's doing, and Eldest Son was grateful. But he remembered the lake in winter and how, in that lifeless season, a man might starve for want of fish. If only there was an easier way to find food! And he raised his thoughts in silent prayer.

'Master of Life, help my people.'

On the fourth day of his fast, Eldest Son felt too weak to go walking, so he stayed in his hut and rested, and waited to see what might come. All day he lay there, and strange imaginings and apparitions danced before his eyes like flickering shadows cast by a fire, now in, now out of his field of vision until he could no longer tell what was real and what was not, for all had the quality of a dream.

At last, as the day drew to its close and the great red Sun dissolved behind the western rim of the world, coating sky and land in gold, Eldest Son thought he saw a figure coming down from the sky, out of the sunset, walking towards him through the velvet haze of twilight. It was a man with golden hair and a plume of silvery feathers, dressed in clothes of green.

The man entered the hut. He spoke to Eldest Son.

'The Master of Life has sent me,' he said, 'in answer to your prayers. I am your guardian spirit, and this is your spirit name: from now on, you are Wunzh. If you wish to help your people, you must first fight with me.'

Fight? How could he fight? the young man thought. He had hardly the strength to stand! But somehow, from somewhere deep within him, Wunzh – as he now was – felt a surge of courage that gave him the power to stand and face his opponent. The pair tussled and wrestled and grappled, first one and then the other seeming to gain the advantage. Suddenly, as Wunzh had almost conceded defeat, the spirit being drew back.

'That is enough,' he said. 'We will resume our fight tomorrow.' And he disappeared by the same way he had come.

It was the same on the fifth day. Wunzh lay in his hut becoming ever fainter with hunger, and as the sun sank in the west and dusk descended, the spirit reappeared. Again, Wunzh felt a surge of courage that gave him strength; somehow, it seemed, the weaker he grew in body, the stronger he became in heart. Once more he wrestled with the spirit being until he could hardly stand, whereupon his adversary called a halt as before, and promised to return the following day to resume the contest.

It was the same on the sixth day. But this time, before the stranger left, he turned to Wunzh and said:

'Tomorrow you will conquer me. Tomorrow I will die. When you see that I am dead, strip off my clothes and bury my body in a place where the earth is soft and free of roots. Do not disturb my grave but care for it: heap fresh soil on it every month and keep it clear of weeds and grass. Do all of this, and you will have the answer to your prayers.' And so saying, he disappeared, melting back into the sunset, back into the sky.

On the seventh and last day of his fast, Wunzh's father came to the hut with some food for him.

'My son,' he said, 'you have completed your trial with honour. Here, take this food, and eat! The Master of Life does not demand your death.'

But weak as he was, Wunzh refused his father's kindness, for what he needed now was not food for the body but food for the spirit. He knew he must hold on to his courage and continue his fast until sunset, when his guardian spirit would come to do battle for the last time.

Everything happened just as the spirit had said. As the fiery Sun slid behind the edge of the world and the shimmering dusk fell like a shower of pollen over the land, there he was, with his golden hair and his waving plume of silvery feathers and his clothes of green.

The pair set to in a ferocious struggle and, as they wrestled and grappled and tussled, limbs and bodies and hair and feathers and fringes blurred together in a whirl of shapes and colours. But at last – and he could hardly believe it – Wunzh had won. His opponent lay lifeless at his feet.

He stripped off the spirit's headdress and clothes and buried his body in the earth, as he had been instructed to, and then he returned to his family, who were overjoyed to see him again. He said nothing of what had happened during his fast, but secretly went to visit the grave he had made and tended it as if it were his own.

Autumn came and went, and then winter, and then the spring with its gentle rain which fell on the place where the spirit lay buried, and then spring blossomed into summer and the benign Sun smiled on the Earth, whispering to all things to grow.

And still Wunzh said nothing of what had happened during his fast.

Then one day, when summer was ripening into autumn and all living things were fertile and fat, Wunzh lead his father to the quiet place when he had undertaken the fast, and there – on the grave of the spirit who had come out of the sky – stood a magnificent plant, with a tall stem and long green leaves and a plume of silvery tassels, and in parcels of overlapping leaves were fat cobs of sweet, juicy, yellow kernels.

'Do you see?' Wunzh said to his father. 'Do you see? This is my guardian spirit. This is Mondawmin ... *Mon-daw-min* – 'corn for all Indians'. From now on, we need never go hungry again for we can grow our own food. In the spring, we will plant the seed corn in the earth, just as I buried Mondawmin's body. In the autumn we will harvest the crop and store it for the winter. This is the gift from the Master of Life – this is his gift to humankind.'

And Wunzh told his father how to strip the ears of corn and how to sow the corn in blocks so that the wind could blow the pollen in the tassels from one plant to the next to make them fertile. He told him, too, how to roast the cobs before the fire, just long enough to brown the outer leaves while keeping the kernels sweet and juicy.

Wunzh and his family then feasted and held a ceremony of thanksgiving, in gratitude to the Great Spirit for his enduring bounteousness. And the knowledge that Wunzh gained on his spirit quest passed on from his family to all the people, for all the generations to come, so that for ever afterwards the Chippewa and Ojibwa honoured him and remembered him as the Father of Indian Corn.

THE BOY WHO BROUGHT THE BUFFALOES

PAWNEE • PLAINS

IT WAS WINTERTIME AND SNOW LAY THICK ON THE GROUND. There were few buffalo to be found and the people had hardly any food left. They had eaten all their *pemmican*, their dried meat, saved from the summer hunt, and all their corn. Now they were having to eat their buffalo-skin robes and moccasins and their *parfleches*, their rawhide cases, just to stay alive. The adults were starving. The little ones were dying. It was a bad, bad time.

But still they kept moving southwards – slowly, for they were very weak – hoping to find the herds, hoping that their luck would change. Every day the scouts would go on ahead, to look out from the highest hills. Every day it was the same.

'What did you see?' the people would eagerly ask when the scouts returned at night.

'Nothing but the snow lying, nothing but the wind crying,' was the inevitable reply.

Now there was among the people a youth of about sixteen years of age. He had been orphaned and had no family in the world. But one of the women, whose husband had been killed by the Pawnees' enemies, the Sioux, and who had two children of her own – a boy and a girl – took pity on the lonely youth and let him live with them. Whenever he managed to find any scraps of food, he would give it to the woman who had become his mother, and she would share it among the four of them. But more often than not there was nothing to be had, and they would all go hungry.

The youth was growing weaker by the day. He could not keep up with the others and one day he found himself so diminished in strength that he could not even help the woman pack up their lodge and place their belongings on the *travois*, the sledge.

'Why should I go on? I am too weak to do the simplest task. Leave me – I will only be a burden to you,' he said, and the woman had not the strength to dissuade him, even though she knew that this meant his almost certain death. With tears in her eyes, she said goodbye to him – 'May Tirawa take pity on you' – and she and her children set off, leaving the youth behind, a small, dark figure alone in the silent snow.

'Well,' he thought, 'I may as well make the best of it. I haven't long left.' And he stoked the small fire that was still burning and spread his hands out over the flames to warm them. Then he settled down to await what he knew would come. Faint from hunger, he soon succumbed to sleep. And in his sleep he had a dream – or at least that is how it seemed.

He dreamed that he woke from his sleep, around the middle of the day, and that he saw two dark shapes in the sky coming towards him, growing larger as they came. They landed on the snow next to him. They were a pair of swans.

They waddled straight up to him, slid their broad, strong wings beneath him, lifted him onto their backs and flew with him, up, up, up, into the blue sky.

And then, in his dream, the youth fell asleep again.

When he next awoke, he was lying on the ground in front of a magnificent lodge, painted with pictures of animals. He tried to stand up, but could not, and managed only with the greatest effort to stumble to the doorway and enter. Inside sat a circle of men, dressed in clothes of the finest beaver skin and buckskin embroidered with quills – great chiefs, warriors, wise men, medicine men. And there, in their midst, was Tirawa, the Creator, the Great Spirit, himself. He wore a robe of the purest white buffalo skin.

'Welcome, my son,' said Tirawa to the amazed youth. 'I have been expecting you.' And he gestured to one of the warriors to give him something to eat. The man took down a *parfleche* sack painted with beautiful patterns, selected some meat from it and cut it, topping it with a slice of fat. This he gave to the new guest.

It was only a small mouthful, hardly enough to revive someone who was starving, the youth thought. But he found that no matter how much he ate of it, the meat and fat stayed exactly the same size.

When the boy was at last satisfied and feeling stronger, Tirawa spoke.

'I have seen the sufferings of your people and I wish to help them. This is what you must do ...' And he gave the youth his instructions. He also gave him a fine new set of clothes. Then he beckoned to one of the warriors: 'Send him home.'

The warrior led the youth outside to where the swans were waiting. He told him to climb back onto their backs. Then he passed his fingers lightly over his eyes, and the youth at once fell asleep again.

He remembered nothing more of what happened. All he knew, when he woke, was that he was alone on the snow. The fire had gone out.

'Who? What? Where am I? Have I been dreaming?' And he pinched himself to see if he was awake, and alive. It hurt – yes; he was both wide-awake and fully alive. Strangely, he felt much stronger, as if he had eaten a hearty meal.

He could see the footprints of his people and the marks of their *travois* poles in the snow, and he hurried after them. He caught up with them that night. He walked through the camp until he found the lodge of his foster mother, and entered it.

'Aaaah!' she screamed when she saw him, staggering backwards. 'Are you a ghost?'

'No, Mother, I am not a ghost. I am more alive than you are. I have returned, with the blessing of Tirawa, to help you.'

He watched as the woman stirred a pot on the fire in the middle of the lodge. 'What are you doing, Mother?' he asked.

'I am going to boil the last little piece of my robe. That is all we have left to eat. After that we will die.'

The youth said nothing, but silently left the lodge. A moment later, he returned.

'Why are you boiling your robe, Mother, when you know there is meat outside?'

Well, thought the woman, hunger and his time alone in the snow must have unhinged his mind. What was this nonsense he was talking? But she went outside to look anyway. And there, looming dark against the white, was the body of a fine, fat buffalo cow.

The woman could not believe her eyes or her luck. She skinned the animal and cooked some of the meat and gave it to her son and her daughter and to the youth, and ate some herself. And next morning, because she had a kind and generous heart, she invited all her relations and friends to share in a meal with her and her family – 'For I have more than I need.'

Oh, and what a feast they had! They had never tasted meat so good. They ate and they ate until their stomachs were full. Then they lit their pipes and let the smoke rise to heaven and offered prayers of gratitude to Tirawa: 'Father, you are great above all.'

While the people were still smoking, the youth called the woman's son over to him.

'Go,' he said, 'to the top of the hill, and tell me what you see.'

So the boy went running, running, running to the top of the hillside. The sun was shining and its rays were glancing off the snow that covered the prairie, blinding him. He shielded his eyes with his hand so that he could see better.

But all he could see was snow, dazzling snow, stretching as far as the horizon.

'I see nothing,' he said to the youth when he returned.

'Go back. You aren't looking hard enough.'

So again the boy went running, running, running to the top of the hillside. He shielded his eyes as before. But again all he could see was a vast expanse of whiteness.

'I see nothing,' he said.

'Go again. You aren't looking hard enough.'

For the third time the boy went running, running, running to the top of the hillside. For the third time he looked. And what did he see?

Buffalo.

Hundreds and hundreds of buffalo, bulls and cows and calves, their black shapes blotting out the snow, darkening the prairie like some great forest on the move. The boy ran screaming back to the camp.

'I have seen them! I have seen the buffalo!'

At once all the men seized their bows and arrows and ran, and the women, with their babies and children, followed with their knives and their *travois* sledges for skinning the beasts and loading the meat. Hampered by the snow, the buffalo could not stampede and the men had an easy kill. They killed enough buffalo to last them until the summer hunt.

Oh, and what a feasting began that day! What a cooking and a drying of meat! What a tanning of hides! What laughter, what songs, what stories! So much joy, so much thankfulness – 'Tirawa, Father, you are great!'

The youth who had been the agent of all this good fortune grew to be a great and wise man among the people. And when the chief – who had up to this time been a woman – died, he became chief in her place and lived well and happily to a ripe old age.

Long may his name be praised.

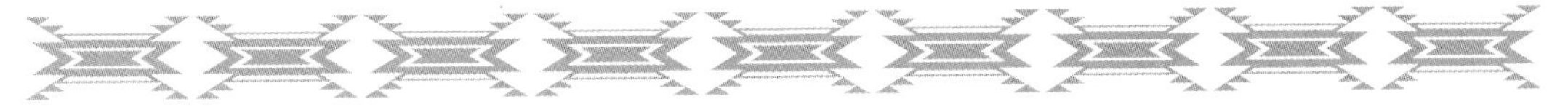

A Buffalo Hunt

George Bird Grinnell lived among the Pawnees for a time, and had first-hand experience of their way of life. The following extract is taken from his account of a buffalo hunt in which he took part in July 1872.

'The scene that we now beheld was such as might have been witnessed here a hundred years ago. Here were eight hundred warriors, stark naked, and mounted on naked animals. Their bows and arrows they held in their hands. Armed with these ancestral weapons, they had become once more the simple children of the plains, about to slay the wild cattle that *Tir-ra'wa* had given them for food....

Each naked Indian seemed a part of his steed, and rose and fell with it in the rhythmic swing of its stride. The plain was peopled with Centaurs. Out over each horse's croup floated the long black hair of his rider, spread out on the wings of the breeze.... We were approaching the top of a high bluff, when the signal was given to halt.... Two or three of the soldiers [warriors of middle age chosen to direct the hunt] rode up nearly to the top of the hill, dismounted and then peered over, and a moment later, at another signal, all mounted and the swift gallop began again. Over the ridge we passed, down the smooth slope, and across a wide level plain, where the prairie dogs and the owls and the rattlesnakes had their home.... But no one took much thought of dog town or horse or possible accident, for the minds of all were upon the next high ridge, behind which we felt sure that the buffalo would be found.

And so it proved.... As we rode slowly up over the ridge, we saw spread out before us a wide valley black with buffalo....

At least a thousand buffalo were lying down in the midst of this amphitheater. Here and there, away from the main herd on the lower hills, were old bulls, singly and by twos and threes, some of them quietly chewing the cud, others sullenly pawing up the dust, or grinding their battered horns into the yellow dirt of the hillsides. Not the slightest notice was taken of us as we rode down the slope at a pace that was almost a run, but still held in check by the soldiers.... We had covered perhaps half the distance between the hilltop and the buffalo, when some of the outlying bulls seemed to observe us, and after looking for a moment or two, these started in rapid flight. This attracted the attention of the herd, and when we were yet half a mile from them, they took the alarm. At once all were on their feet. For a moment they gazed bewildered at the dark line that was sweeping toward them, and then, down went

every huge head and up flew every little tail, and the herd was off in a headlong stampede for the opposite hills. As they sprang to their feet, the oldest man of the soldiers, who was riding in the center of the line, turned back toward us, and uttered a shrill *Loo'ah!* It was the word we had waited for.

Like an arrow from a bow each horse darted forward. Now all restraint was removed, and each man might do his best. What had been only a wild gallop became a mad race. Each rider hoped to be the first to reach the top of the opposite ridge, and to turn the buffalo back into the valley, so that the surround might be completely successful.... This was the first object of the chase, for in a stampede, the cows and young are always in the lead, the bulls bringing up the rear. This position is not taken from chivalric motives on the part of the males, but simply because they cannot run so fast as their wives and children. Bulls are never killed when cows and heifers can be had.

Back came the herd, and I soon found myself in the midst of a throng of buffalo, horses and Indians.... It was far more interesting to watch the scene than to take part in it, and I soon rode to a little knoll from which I could overlook the whole plain. Many brown bodies lay stretched upon the ground, and many more were dashing here and there, closely attended by relentless pursuers. It was sad to see so much death, but the people must have food, and none of this meat would be wasted.

Before I turned my horse's head toward the camp, the broad disk of the setting sun had rested on the tops of the western bluffs, and tipped their crests with fire. His horizontal beams lit up with a picturesque redness the dusky forms which moved about over the valley. Up the ravines and over the hills were stringing long lines of squaws [Indian women], leading patient ponies, whose backs were piled high with dark dripping meat, and with soft shaggy skins. Late into the night the work continued and the loads kept coming into the camp. About the flickering fires in and before the lodges there was feasting and merriment. Marrowbones were tossed among the red embers, calf's head was baked in the hot earth, fat ribs were roasted, *ka'-wis* [small intestines filled with chopped buffalo meat] boiled, and *boudins* [blood puddings] eaten raw. With laughter and singing and story telling and dance the night wore away.

Over the plain where the buffalo had fallen, the gray wolf was prowling and, with the coyote, the fox and the badger, tore at the bones of the slain. When day came, the golden eagle and the buzzard perched upon the naked red skeletons, and took their toll. And far away to the southward, a few frightened buffalo, some of which had arrows sticking in their sore sides, were cropping the short grass of the prairie.'

GHOSTS AND THE SUPERNATURAL

How Death Came Into the World

PAWNEE • PLAINS

Tirawa had made the world and it was good. But there was still some work to do so Tirawa sent Lightning down to add the finishing touches. In his hand Lightning carried a bag given to him by Bright Star, lord of the elements. The bag contained all the stars of heaven and something else too – all the storms, all the wild winds and all the raging tempests. They jostled and bumped about inside the bag like cats in a sack. Lightning was in charge of them all.

He had a wonderful time poking and prodding around in the new world which Tirawa had made. He stretched out his long, crooked arms to touch the mountaintops. He fingered the branches of the trees with his long, sinewy hands. He crackled with laughter over the prairies.

When at last he had been to all four quarters of the world and seen all there was to see, he put down the bag he had been carrying and took out the stars. He began to arrange them carefully in the sky. A big one here. A little one there. An artistic placement of others in-between, forming a constellation. Lightning became so absorbed in what he was doing – and he had hundreds of stars still to place – that he forgot all about the bag lying on the ground nearby.

Among the stars which he had already set in the sky was Coyote Cheater, so called because he fools Coyote into thinking he is the Morning Star. As well as being deceitful, Coyote Cheater was also greedy. He knew that Bright Star had power over the elements, and he wanted that power for himself – he wanted the bag of storms. But how to get it? He couldn't reach it himself, stuck up there in the sky as he was. Someone else would have to do his thieving for him.

It was then that Coyote Cheater spotted Wolf, loping alone through the forest.

'Psst!' he hissed. 'Up here!'

Wolf looked around. Was someone trying to attract his attention?

'Here – up in the sky!'

Wolf looked up.

'Yes – I'm the one that was calling you. Now look – I have a little errand I want you to do for me. And of course, there'll be something in it for you ...' And with false promises of rewards to come, Coyote Cheater persuaded Wolf to steal the bag of storms.

Wolf sneaked up to where the bag lay and, with all his hunter's stealth, snatched it up in his jaws and made off with it before Lightning even realized it was gone. Wolf went lumbering back through the forest, back to where Coyote Cheater was waiting, with the bag bumping along behind him, over stones, over logs, under branches, over bushes. Wolf was nearly there. He could hardly wait to claim his reward!

It was just as he was leaping over a fallen tree-trunk that it happened. The bag snagged on a jutting branch and split open.

All the storms and all the wild winds and all the raging tempests came roaring out. They looked for their master, Lightning. And when they could not find him, and when they realized that they had been kidnapped and discovered who had done it, they set upon foolish Wolf and beat him and battered him until he was dead. And so it was that Wolf became the first living creature to die.

That is how Death came into the world. And it will never leave until the sun turns black and the moon turns red and the Star of Death rules the sky, and when that time comes the spirits of the dead will be made into stars and will travel the Wolf Trail, Milky Way, for that is the Souls' highway across heaven.

THE FLYING HEAD

IROQUOIS • NORTHEAST

East of the river and west of the sea, north of the marshes and south of the snow, there once lived a brave young woman who was seldom, if ever, afraid of anything. She did not fear the voice of the thunder, or the lightning crack, or the snake that bites underfoot, or the strange whisperings of the woods or the shadows that flit and flicker in dark places. More remarkably – and this is the wonder of it – she did not even fear the flying heads, those body-less spectres that ride the storm and come at night, matted locks a-streaming, glaring eyes a-glinting, yellow fangs a-snapping, in search of human flesh. And that is why, when one of these monsters was seen darting through the treetops one wild and turbulent evening, the brave young woman decided not to run away like everyone else but to stay right where she was.

'But it's *flying head!*' her mother protested. 'You must hide!'

'But it's a *flying head!*' her father objected. 'It will eat you up if you stay!'

'But it's a *flying head!*' her husband insisted. 'You cannot confront it alone!'

'Someone's got to do it,' said the brave young woman, who was seldom, if ever, afraid of anything, as she sat by the fire in the longhouse, rocking her baby on her knee. Seeing that there was no arguing with her – she had always been stubborn, her mother thought – her family left her on her own to seek their own safety.

Well, the young woman sat and waited. She knew it wouldn't be long. She stoked up the fire and placed some stones on it, to heat. She crooned a lullaby to her baby, *hmmm-mmm, tra-la-la-la.*

Then she heard it. The swoosh of the swishing hair. The click-clack of the snapping jaws. The sniffing of the huge nose, scenting flesh. The drip-drop of the slavering mouth.

The flying head had entered the longhouse and was hovering right behind her, leering and salivating.

The brave young woman took no notice. Instead, using a forked stick, she picked up one of the stones from the fire, which glowed red-hot by now, and pretended to eat it.

'Mmmm ...' She licked her lips. 'Now that *is* good! This is the most delicious food I've ever tasted – better than sweet berries, better than fat meat, better than anything!' And she helped herself to another stone, slipping the first secretly out of sight behind her back.

What was this? The flying head was intrigued. It would have eaten the young

woman but now it wondered: could there be something better even than human flesh? Greed proving more powerful than common sense, it opened it jaws wide, clamped them over the mound of red-hot stones, and swallowed them in a single gulp.

'Aieeee! Ahhhh! Owwww!' The flying head screamed with agony as the stones hissed on its dripping tongue and seared its throat as they went down. It took off, hurtling out through the doorway and into the forest, where it thrashed wildly about in the throes of its pain. Then it was off again, over the treetops, over the mountains, over the plains, to who-knows-where, for in that village no flying head was ever seen again.

When its screams were no more than an echo on the wind and the people realized that it was safe to come out, they came running back. 'You saved us!' they cried. 'We knew that only you could do it – and you did!'

The brave young woman who was seldom, if ever, afraid of anything continued to sit by the fire, rocking her baby on her knee. 'Well,' she said, 'someone had to.'

FALSE FACES

The 'flying head' described in the story of the same name was one of the Iroquois spirits known as the False Faces – disembodied heads with streaming hair and large eyes who travelled through the air, frightening the unwary. The False Face Society, who were an Iroquois group and one of many such Native American mystical societies or brotherhoods, invoked these spirits in their ceremonies. Members would perform healing rituals wearing carved and decorated wooden masks which represented the False Faces and were supernaturally charged with their power. They also carried turtle rattles – made from snapping-turtle shells with hickory handles – to scare away evil spirits.

There were different categories of mask, each with its own associated legend. The most important of these concerned a being known as Old Broken Nose, who had his facial features distorted when he challenged the supremacy of the Creator. He was subsequently made to roam the perimeter of the world, curing people of their illnesses, and in this role was referred to as the Great Doctor.

Performance of the Society's rituals kept the masks supernaturally potent. When not in use, they had to be 'fed' with offerings of tobacco.

BLUE JAY AND IOI

CHINOOK • NORTHWEST COAST

ONE NIGHT THE GHOST PEOPLE SET OUT TO BUY A WIFE. They chose Ioi, the sister of Blue Jay the master trickster. She was married to a dead man that same night. In the morning, when Blue Jay came to see her, she was gone. In her place was a pile of shells, her bride price. He waited for her to return – a week, a month, a year – and then he decided to go and find her.

'Do you know the place where ghosts live?' he asked the trees.

'No, we do not.' The trees shook their leafy heads.

'Do you know the place where ghosts live?' he asked the birds.

'No, we do not.' The birds chirped and twittered their denial.

'Do you know the place where ghosts live?' he asked the animals.

'No, we do not.' The animals bellowed and squeaked their reply.

Blue Jay was getting nowhere. He sat down and thought.

'I know where it is.' Blue Jay look around. He saw an old, gnarled log in front of him. 'I'll take you there,' it said.

So Blue Jay climbed on his tough, rutted back and the log, his magical guide, carried him to the place where ghosts live.

What Blue Jay saw was a large and silent village. There was no sign of life anywhere except for a column of smoke that rose from the smoke-hole of a magnificent cedar-wood lodge at the furthest end.

Blue Jay entered it. 'My brother! My dearest brother!' It was Ioi, his long-lost sister, who threw her arms about his neck. 'Welcome, welcome! Now are you just visiting, or are you staying – are you dead?' The questions tumbled out of her.

'No, of course, I'm not dead. I've just come to see you.'

'Well, it is a pleasure to see you again. Now let me introduce you to my new relations. This is my husband and this is my mother-in-law.

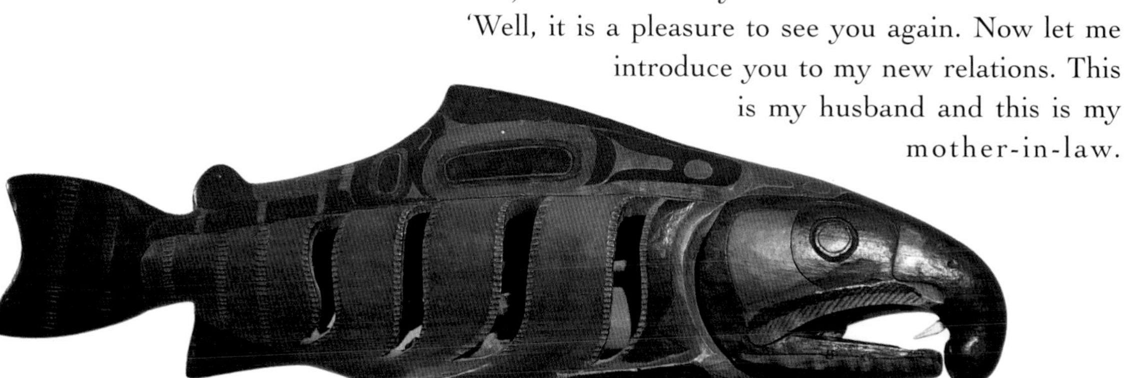

Oh, and this is my father-in-law and my sister in marriage.' On and on she went, through her whole extended family. But all Blue Jay could see were piles of bones. His sister's relatives were no more than skeletons, heaped about the place.

As usual, Ioi was talking nonsense – living among the dead seemed to have done nothing to improve her fanciful mind. 'Ioi is always telling lies,' Blue Jay thought.

But as darkness fell and night came on, the bones were reanimated. Jawbones yawned, vertebrae straightened, femurs and patellas unwound, tibias stretched, phalanges wriggled, thoraxes widened, and bones came together with bones as the skeletons reformed themselves and took on a semblance of life.

'It is time to go fishing,' said Ioi to Blue Jay. 'Go with that boy over there – he is a cousin of my husband. But just behave yourself! Keep your voice down when you talk to him. Ghosts don't like loud noises.'

Blue Jay joined the throng of the dead and climbed into the ghost-boy's canoe with him. As they paddled down the river, all the ghosts began to sing. It was a good tune. Blue Jay sang along, too ... *hey-oh, hi-oh, hey-oh, ho* ... The song swayed back and forth to the slap of the paddles. Blue Jay was really getting into the swing of it now. Carried away by the hypnotic rhythm, he raised his voice higher ... higher ... higher.

Suddenly, he became aware that he was the only one singing. All the ghosts had fallen silent. And when he looked back into his canoe, he saw that the ghost-boy had turned into bones again.

Blue Jay waited. This time when he looked back again, there was the ghost-boy as before, his fishing net on his knee.

'Where do you find the fish?' he whispered in the smallest voice possible.

'Further down the river,' replied the ghost-boy.

'What did you say? I didn't hear you. Speak up – WHERE DO YOU FIND THE FISH?' Again the boy was turned to bones. Bones, flesh, bones, flesh, and all just by altering the volume of one's voice! It was exactly the kind of game that Blue Jay liked. It kept him pleasantly occupied until they reached the fishing site.

Blue Jay lowered his net into the water. When he drew it up, it was bursting with a rich catch – of wet leaves! He shook the net and some of the leaves fell into the canoe. The ghost-boy gathered them up.

Blue Jay lowered his net a second time and again, when he drew it up, it was brimful of leaves and, for good measure, a branch or two as well. As before, the ghost-boy gathered up all the leaves that fell into the canoe.

Blue Jay tried a third time. More leaves! And a fourth time. A pair of branches!

Blue Jay was disgusted. Were there no fish in these waters? What a wasted journey he had had. He did notice, however, that the ghost-boy had caught nothing either. In fact, he had not even attempted to fish, but had just sat watching and collecting up the fallen leaves.

Then the company paddled for home.

'Well,' said Blue Jay to Ioi, 'that was a waste of time. I didn't catch a single fish! All I caught were a load of leaves and branches. I threw most of them back in the water. '

'What do you mean, you threw them back in the water?' shrieked his sister. 'Don't you know that the branches were salmon and the leaves were trout?'

She was doing it again – talking nonsense. 'Ioi is always telling lies,' Blue Jay thought.

But when he looked back towards the canoe resting on the riverbank, it was full of a wriggling, silver mass of fish. These were the 'leaves' and 'branches' he had caught and which the ghost-boy was now unloading.

Blue Jay began to enjoy his stay. The ghost people were the perfect target for his particular brand of humour. His favourite practical joke – and he did so love a good joke – was to swap the bones around, placing the skull of a child on the skeleton of a man, or a man's skull on a child's neck. Or he might give an old man the legs of a baby, or a woman the legs of a man. Then he would wait, with barely suppressed giggles, for night to fall. And it was worth the wait for what a sight they were when they came alive, with all their bits and pieces jumbled up! The child with the man's skull tottered about, its enlarged head lolling on its shoulders; the old man with the legs of a baby kept falling over because the legs had not yet learned to walk; and the woman with the legs of a man swaggered about as if she were the bravest buck, the lustiest lad in all the village.

It was too much! How Blue Jay laughed! He held his sides. He rolled on the ground. He hadn't played such a good trick in years.

When he went out with the ghost fishermen, there was more fun to be had by reducing them to bones with a shout. Blue Jay was so glad he had come to this place. He was having the time of his life.

THE LITTLE PEOPLE

It may be surprising to learn that, in addition to huge giants, Native American tribes also believed in 'Little People' who bear an often uncanny similarity to those diminutive supernaturals who inhabit the Otherworld of European lore.

For the Algonquian Indians of the Northeast they were the *May-may-gway-shi*, rock-dwellers who lived in caves or crevices by the waterside. They often stole fish, of which they were especially fond, from the Indians' nets, but if they were pursued, they paddled their stone canoes straight into the rock face and disappeared. Only the most powerful shamans were capable of entering the rock to obtain some of their magic – which was highly potent – in exchange for tobacco. If proof of their existence is needed, it may be seen in the prehistoric rock carvings and paintings of North America: these are the work of the *May-may-gway-shi* whose red handprints may sometimes be seen on the rock face.

Plateau and Basin tribes had a dwarf spirit who was master of the animals, and who took the form of a little green man. His invisible arrows caused sickness in both people and animals. Like Rumpelstiltskin, his name was a secret and it was taboo to speak it.

Canotina or Canotili of the Lakota and Dakota Sioux of the Plains was a dwarf of the trees, who waited for lone hunters and caused people to become lost in the forest. Sightings of him were bad omens, for they signified the imminent death of a close relative.

Likewise in the Southeast, sightings of the Cherokee Little People were portents of death. Described as being about 75 cm (2 ½ ft) tall, naked, and with long hair, these beings had much in common with their Celtic counterparts across the water. They were of unpredictable temperament and could be kind, helpful, mischievous or downright malevolent; they stole human children; and their magic food, if taken out of its supernatural context, crumbled to dust. Those who returned from visiting them were warned not to speak of their experience for three weeks; if they disobeyed this prohibition – a temptation which usually proved impossible to resist – they died soon after.

The traits of the Little People of North America find strong parallels in the fairy lore of Europe, a commonality which suggests a universal mythological archetype.

But others were less happy. The ghost people did not see the funny side, nor share Blue Jay's sense of humour. They did not like being made the butt of his jokes, and they began to complain loudly.

'He has outstayed his welcome,' Ioi's husband said to her. 'Your brother will have to go.'

'You have to go,' said Ioi to Blue Jay. And she gave him five buckets of water to take with him. 'The journey home is full of dangers for you will encounter burning prairies on the way. But you will be safe as long as you do what I say: do not pour any of the water from the buckets until you reach the fourth prairie.'

What nonsense was she talking this time? 'Ioi is always telling lies,' thought Blue Jay, but he took the buckets anyway and, after saying a warm goodbye to his sister, set off for home.

When Blue Jay came to the first prairie, there was no fire, but it was very hot. 'I was right,' he said to himself. 'There is no fire here. Ioi is always telling lies.' But he did notice how dry the grass was. 'The grass is thirsty,' he thought and, ignoring his sister's advice, he poured out some of the water to cool it.

When he came to the second prairie, he saw that a quarter of it was on fire. He poured out more water to quench the flames.

When he came to the third prairie, he saw that half of it was ablaze. He poured out more water to put out the fire.

When he came to the fourth prairie, he saw that three-quarters of it was burning. 'Ioi is always telling lies,' he reminded himself as he poured out the last of the water on the fire.

And that is why, when he came to the fifth prairie which was completely ablaze, he had no water left to put out the flames which engulfed him and burned him to death.

'*Keek, keek, keek!*' Ioi heard her brother calling to her from far, far away. 'My brother is dead,' she said to her husband. 'I will go to fetch him home.'

And so she climbed into her canoe and set off across the river to find him.

And when she did, it was as if his eyes had been opened. Her canoe, in which she paddled him back over the water and which he had once thought was a hulk full of holes, he saw to be a fine craft. The ghost people in the village, whom he had once thought were mere bags of bones, he saw to be bonny children and buxom women and sturdy men.

'But they are beautiful, so beautiful,' Blue Jay said to his sister. 'I never knew.'

'You are seeing with the eyes of the dead,' she replied, 'for now you are one of us.'

And Ioi was not telling lies.

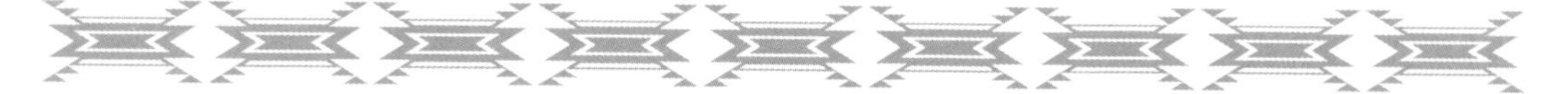

THE BOY WHO RAN WITH THE WOLVES

CHIPPEWA-OJIBWA • NORTHEAST

THERE WAS ONCE A MAN WHO HAD A WIFE AND THREE CHILDREN – a son, a daughter and a little boy. Their wigwam lay in the forest, far away from the village and its people, for the father knew the treacherous ways of humankind and wished to protect his family from them.

One day the father grew sick. He knew he was dying. He called his wife and children to him. 'My dearest wife,' he began, 'companion of all my days. I am called to the Land of Souls. Soon you, too, will join me there. Then you, my children, will have no one else in the world. Promise me this before I die: promise that you will always love each other and that you, my son and my daughter, will look after your young brother for he is a child, and small and weak.'

'I promise,' said the son.

'I promise,' said the daughter.

And the little boy, not understanding the grave issues being discussed above his head, gazed on with his round child's eyes.

Then the father, having heard the words he wished to hear, breathed his last breath and his soul left his body and went to join the ancestors.

One moon passed, then two, then three, and at the end of eight moons the mother, just as her husband had predicted, also sickened and died.

Now the brother and sister were truly alone in the world, with their little brother. But they remembered the promise they had made, and the elder brother went out hunting and the sister cooked the game he caught and sewed and cared for the wigwam. In this way they maintained their little family and stayed well fed and warm.

And then the snows came and covered the world in a canopy of white and the animals went to ground in their burrows and dens and all the forest was silent, and in their wigwam brother and sister and little brother stayed by the fire to keep warm. 'Coo, coo, hush, hush, little one,' the sister crooned as she sang the boy to sleep.

Two moons went by, then three and spring arrived and the snow melted and clear water ran in the streams and green shoots pushed up out of the earth. Another moon and the trees frothed with blossom and the birds sang and the air was warm, and the elder brother looked about him and in his breast his heart hardened.

'The birds in the trees have life and the animals on the ground. What life have I, hidden away here from the rest of the world?' he thought. And he revealed his unhappiness to his sister.

'I understand how you feel,' she said, 'but if we think only of ourselves, what about our little brother? What about the promise we made to look after him?'

But the elder brother would not listen and picked up his bow and arrows and left, to seek the village and people and busyness and life.

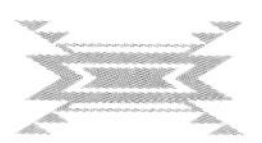

Now the sister was alone with her little brother in the wigwam in the forest. The leaves on the trees turned to gold and red, and then the winter came with the snow, covering the world in a canopy of white, and then the spring with its joyful surge of blossom and birdsong. But the elder brother did not return, and the sister had to take on his tasks as well as her own, hunting and making fires and cooking and sewing and working her fingers to the bone. All this she did in the solitude of the forest, so that she felt burdened and bitter and in her breast her heart hardened.

'What kind of life do I have here? I do nothing but work all day and I am so lonely, with no companion to share my days. If I lived in the village, I would be among people and be married by now, with a husband and family of my own.'

So she gathered up a load of wood for the fire and a large stock of food, and said to her little brother: 'I am going to the village to find our brother. Here is food and firewood to feed you and keep you warm until I get back.' Then she left.

And she did find her brother. He was married and living in the village, and seemed very happy. 'Come,' he said. 'Join us. Life is good here.' And so the sister stayed and in time she was courted by a young man and became his wife. As summer ripened into autumn and autumn slid into the sleep of winter, she thought less and less about her little brother alone in the forest, and how she had meant to return.

The boy, meanwhile, managed to keep himself alive by making the fire as his sister had taught him and cooking and eating the food she had left. But the store gradually ran out, and the boy had to leave the wigwam to gather berries and dig up roots, for this was all he could find to eat. He survived in this way through the summer and autumn. But then the winter came, bringing snow and freezing wind, and the boy shivered with cold and hunger and huddled for shelter among the trees. He took to scavenging,

picking up any scraps of meat or bone that the wolves had left. In time, he grew quite bold and would follow the pack and sit to one side watching them as they devoured their latest kill. The animals knew he was there.

'Brother Wolf,' said one of the beasts to another. 'Do you see that human child?'

'Yes, indeed, Brother Wolf, I do.'

'He is starving.'

'I see it. Let him share our food.'

And so it was, throughout that long, cold winter, that they allowed him part of every kill they made and it was the kindness of the animals that saved him from death – and so it was that the boy began to run with the wolves.

One spring day, after the snow had gone and the ice on the lake had melted, the elder brother went out fishing in his canoe. It was peaceful, out there on the water, and he began to contemplate his life. It had been good to him, he thought. He had a wife and several children, all the wealth he needed, and was well respected in his community. He felt secure in his contentment. Yes, life was good, very good.

It was then that he heard it, breaking the stillness. It was the cry of a child, and the ghostliest sound he had ever heard, echoing over the water. It sent a shiver down his spine. But what child could there be out here, so far from all human life?

The elder brother paddled as fast as he could towards the shore, which was the direction from which the sound had come. There it was again! He heard it more clearly this time. What was that it was saying?

My brother, oh, my brother, I am turning into a wolf …

And then he saw an incredible sight. Could it be true? Was it really him – the little brother whom he had abandoned in order to seek a better life for himself? Yes, it was – but there was something different about him, something animal, elemental. While his head, arms and torso were those of a normal human child, his legs were covered with silver hair, he had paws instead of feet, and between his legs a tail dangled.

The elder brother looked on in horror as the child tilted back his head to release his song once more …

My brother, oh, my brother, I am turning into a wolf … after which he howled as a wolf does, and his call was answered by a chorus of other howls from unseen throats on all sides until the lake and the shore and the wooded slopes rang with the song of the wolves.

The elder brother scrambled ashore. He had to save his little brother. None of this would be happening if he had stayed with him, he knew that now, and he was overcome with remorse and pity. This was his chance to make up for the wrong he had done, for the promise he had broken.

'Do you not know me, little brother? Come to me, come,' he called out as he lunged desperately at the wolf-boy and tried to catch him in his arms. But the wolf-boy side-stepped him and ran away. The elder brother chased after him, but the closer he got the more like a wolf the boy became …

My brother, oh, my brother, I am turning into a wolf …

In the end not a vestige of humanity was left and the boy was a wolf from head to foot. Raising his voice in one last howl, he bounded after the waiting pack, and disappeared into the forest.

Defeated, the elder brother paddled his canoe wearily back across the lake and returned home to tell his sister the sad tale.

That day and every day for the rest of their lives, they thought about what they had done; neither could forget how, through their own selfishness, they had broken their promise to their dying father and abandoned their own brother in the forest. The elder brother grieved and the sister cried, and so numerous were her tears that they could have filled a river. And it was in the quiet moments of their days – when the sister was plaiting her own children's hair, perhaps, or weaving a mat of rushes; when the brother was out tracking the deer, or sitting smoking tobacco – that memories of their lost brother would flood unbidden into their minds and overwhelm them with unbearable sorrow.

Oh, my brother, oh, my sister, I have turned into a wolf ...

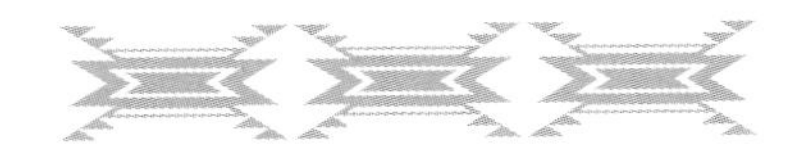

The Wooden Doll

IROQUOIS • NORTHEAST

THERE WAS ONCE A MAN who lived alone with his wife in a bark-covered house in the woods, far away from the nearest village. Often, in the day, the man would go out hunting and trapping, and his wife would go with him. She seemed to bring him luck, for when she was with him he never came home empty-handed. But then the woman found that she had too much to do in and around the house, so she stayed behind while her husband went out. She tended her patch of maize and beans and squash, and stretched and tanned the skin of the deer her husband had killed, and mended and sewed, and made the fire and cooked the meals. And the husband soon noticed, now that he was going out alone, that he caught much less game.

Things went on in this way for some time, but then the wife became ill. Her husband cared for her with the greatest tenderness, for she was all his life to him. He soothed her fevered brow and brought her healing herbs. 'How do you feel, my dearest? Are you better yet? Please do not die – do not leave me here alone.' But it was no use. The sickness was more powerful than his love and his will, and in the end she succumbed to it and died.

The man was distraught with grief. He wept

and wailed over his dead wife's body. 'How can I go on without you? You were my eyes, my ears, my hands, my heart, you were my very breath.' But no amount of tears could bring her back to life, so he dug a grave and placed her in it, returning her body to the Earth who is our mother.

And the world went on as if she had never been. The Sun shone, the birds sang, the wild berries and nuts fattened on the bushes, the fish swam in the lakes and streams, and the man had to make the best of what was left of his life. Now he had not only his own work to do but also all the jobs that had been done by his wife, and at night he often went to bed exhausted. But it was not that which bothered him most. It was the loneliness. The aching emptiness inside him gnawed away at his being, in his waking moments and in sleep, and would not let him be.

In the end he could stand it no longer. So he fetched a wooden log, about the same length and width as the human body, and began to chip and whittle it away and to carve it into the replica of a woman who looked exactly like his dead wife. Then he took some of his wife's clothes, which he had never thrown away – her beaded shirt with its floral pattern, her beaded leggings, and her soft moccasins – and dressed the doll in them. And he sat the doll down by the fire, in exactly the place his wife used to sit.

'There, there,' he said soothingly. 'You will be all right. Now just you wait until I get back – I won't be long!' And, picking up his bow and arrows, he went out.

When he returned later, the wooden doll was sitting where he had left her. 'Look what I have brought us! A fat rabbit! This will fill our bellies.' And he lit the fire and skinned the rabbit and cooked it. But the wooden doll said nothing.

Things went on in this way for some time. When the man returned at the end of the day from his forays into the forest, or from sowing or harvesting the crops, the doll was always waiting for him, in the place where he had left her. He took care of her as if she were a living, breathing being, brushing off any ashes which had blown onto her from the fire, and changing her clothes to keep her fresh and clean. 'There you are, you'll feel better now.' And after he had eaten, he liked to sit by the fire and talk to her, and tell her of all the ordinary or wonderful or funny things he had seen during his day. And sometimes, just sometimes, if he half-closed his eyes and let himself dream a little, he could almost imagine that his wife was there beside him by the fire, chatting and laughing and exchanging stories as they used to do in the old days.

Then, one evening as he was returning home, the man saw smoke rising from the house. And as he drew nearer, he saw that fresh firewood had been piled up outside and inside a bright fire was burning. Who could have done this thing? There was no one there except the wooden doll, sitting waiting for him in the place where he had left her, and the man was greatly puzzled.

The next day it was the same, only this time there was not only fresh wood and a welcoming fire but meat in the pot as well, almost ready to be eaten. The man searched everywhere for signs of the person who had done this, but could find no one except for the wooden doll who sat, as usual, where she always did by the fire. He was even more puzzled.

The next day he decided to alter his habits a little, and came home earlier than normal so that he might catch out the person who had been taking care of him and his home, and thank them. And as he approached the house, he saw a woman entering it with wood on her shoulders for the fire. He ran to the house as fast as he could and burst in through the doorway. And when he looked at the spot where the wooden doll usually sat, he saw that she was gone ... and in the place where she had been sat his smiling wife instead.

'Oh, my dearest, my beloved! You are alive! You have come back to me.' The man could hardly breathe so great was his joy, and he rushed towards his wife in order to take her in his arms.

'NO!' she shouted. 'Stop! The Great Spirit saw your sorrow and took pity on you. That is why I have been allowed to return. But you must not touch me until we have seen the rest of our people. If you do, I shall die a second time, and you will never see me again.'

This was a harsh condition, but what could the husband do but agree? He had his wife back, and that was all that mattered.

They soon fell into their old life again, and the sorrow that had etched itself on the husband's face, and made him look old before his time, melted away like snow in springtime, so that now a healthy, youthful bloom flushed his cheeks and he looked, once more, like a young man.

Things went on in this way for some time, and many moons passed. And then the husband said to his wife: 'It is not natural for us to live as we do. You are whole now and strong and recovered from death. It is time for you to meet our people. Then we can live together as man and wife, as the Great Spirit intended. Come, let us go.'

The wife agreed and so they packed up and made ready to leave. They took some *pemmican*, a mix of dried meat and fat, for the journey, and skins to keep them warm and such other provisions as they might need, for it would take six days to reach the village.

They walked and they walked and they walked. One day went by, two days, then three, then four. Now it was the fifth and they had only one more day to travel before they reached their destination. It began to snow. They were tired and cold and hungry. So they stopped, put up a makeshift shelter, made a fire, cooked and ate some food, then wrapped themselves in their skins and prepared to sleep.

Cocooned in the warmth of the fur, the husband looked over at his wife, so near him and yet so far. It had been a long time – too long – since he had held her, or stroked her hair, or kissed or caressed her. Surely the Great Spirit did not wish it to be this way, that a man might not be a husband to his wife? They were only a day from the village. One sunset, one sunrise away. All he wanted was to give her a hug, that was all – a hug, nothing more. Surely the Great Spirit would not begrudge him that, not now? And he reached out his arms to his wife.

'No!' she cried, intercepting him. 'Remember – you must not touch me until we have seen our people!'

But the husband would not listen and gathered his wife to him and held her close. 'Oh, my dearest one! How long I have waited to hold you!' And he buried his face in her hair and felt its softness and breathed in her old familiar smell.

But in his arms his wife changed – he could feel it quite clearly – and grew stiff and hard and cold. And when he drew back to look at her, to ask her why she was so unresponsive, he saw that what he held in his arms was no longer his wife. What he held was a wooden doll.

With an anguished cry of rage and despair, he flung the lifeless figure from him. Then he ran and he ran, stumbling and staggering and struggling through the thickening snow, like a man driven to the edge of madness, all the way to the village.

'Help me! Help me! It's my wife! And it's all my fault. I didn't listen, I disobeyed her. She's out there, in the snow ... come and see, come and see!' And the whole story came tumbling out.

Some of the villagers thought he was mad. 'See how he raves? These are not the words of a sane man. He has been out in the snow too long. It has turned his head.'

But others were intrigued by what he told them, and went with him to see if what he said was true. And when they arrived at the spot where he had last seen his wife, there lay the wooden doll, where he had thrown her. Next to her, in the unblemished snow, were two sets of footprints. One set belonged to the husband. The other set was smaller, daintier, more feminine, and matched the feet of the wooden doll exactly.

The villagers exchanged glances. 'He speaks the truth,' they whispered to each other, and looked on the man with pity and a little fear, too, as one might look on someone who has borne more than his share of suffering in this world and has been changed irrevocably by it.

The husband, of course, saw none of this for he was blinded by despair. Instead, he just turned silently on his heel and left, walking off in the direction from which he had come.

And he never ceased grieving all the days of his life.

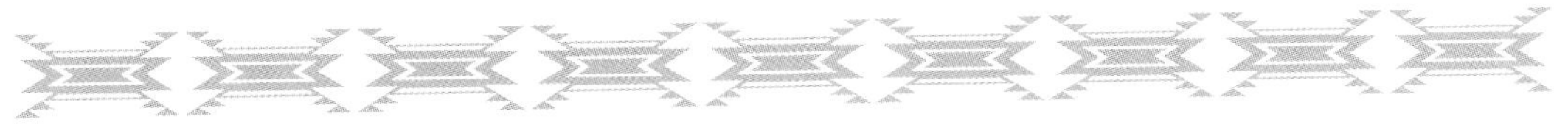

ALGONQUIAN Peoples of the Sub-Arctic and Northeast region, a vast area where life was often dangerous and precarious. Mythology served to reassure people that by correct action they could achieve some influence over the forces of nature. Other tribes from this region include the CREE, IROQUOIS and CHIPPEWA.

BLACKFEET A tribe from the heartland of Native America, the Great Plains. This is the land of vast horizons where proud warriors hunted the buffalo. The wide blue skies were held sacred, embodying the creative force of the universe. The Plains Indians tribes include the OMAHA, SIOUX and PAWNEE, so well known from countless Westerns.

CHEROKEE A tribe from the culturally diverse Southeast. With Mexican and South American influences, this region is famous for the extraordinary Serpent Mound and the ancient pyramid city of Cahokia. The YUCHI tribe also live in the Southeast.

CHINHOOK Running to the southwest of the Sub-Arctic is the Northwest Coast, home to the Chinook, as well as the TLINGIT, TSIMSHIAN and MAKAH tribes. Fronting the Pacific, the peoples of this land are whalers and fishermen, and their stories reflect the close relationship with the sea.

FLATHEAD To the east and southeast of the Northwest Coast area lies the Plateau and Basin region, home of the Flathead and NEZ PERCÉ tribes. The landscape, climate and culture of this region are all diverse. The mythology reflects a common belief in the sacredness of all things, animate or inanimate.

HOPI These people are from the Southwest, a region that includes the Grand Canyon and the desert. The HOPI, ZUNI and PIMA tribes are descended from the cliff-dwelling ANASAZI and are called DESERT PUEBLO. Snakes and rain-making rituals are important in the mythology of the Southwest.

INUIT Inhabitants of the Arctic region of North America and descendants of the Eskimos who migrated from Asia around 10,000 years ago, they retain a strong resemblance to their Mongolian ancestors. Their stories, like their environment, are harsh and stark in character. The ALEUT and YUPIK peoples also inhabit this region.

NAVAJO Descendants of the Athapaskan-speaking nomadic peoples who travelled southward from their original homeland in the Sub-Arctic. They settled near the Pueblo Indians and became known as the Navajo.

PUEBLO A Spanish word that means 'people', it is also used to describe a village made of multi-storeyed adobe (sun-dried brick) buildings, as well as the Indian peoples who lived there.

INDEX

PICTURE CREDITS & ACKNOWLEDGEMENTS

Front cover: Navaho blanket showing two 'holy people' with the sacred maize plant, which was their gift to mortals (Schindler Collection, New York/WFA)
Back cover: A shaman's storage chest carved with a face representing the Moon, from the Northwest Coast region (Provincial Museum, Victoria, British Columbia, Canada, no. 1564/WFA)
p.2 Ceremonial crest headdress, Northwest Coast (Museum of the American Indian, Haye Foundation, New York, USA/WFA)
p.3 Cochiti (Pueblo) painted drum (© Ben Connor) (Maxwell Museum of Anthropology, University of New Mexico)
p.8 Plains Indian war-medicine shield depicting the Moon, Crow 19th c., Montana (Field Museum of Natural History, Chicago/WFA)
p.10 Skeena River, British Columbia, Canada and the mountain of Stekya-den near Hazelton (WFA)
p.11 Haida mask said to represent the Moon (National Museum of Man, Ottawa /WFA);
p.12 The border of Montana and Wyoming (WFA)
p.13 and p.127 Samples of maize, squashes and beans – the three sisters of the woodland Indians, Richmond, Virginia (© Colin Taylor)
p.15 Hopi kachina doll (© Ben Connor) (Maxwell Museum of Anthropology, University of New Mexico)
p.16 Cliff Palace ruin, Mesa Verde National Park, Colorado (© Ben Connor)
pp.18–19 Pima Point looking east up the canyon – Mojave Point, South Rim, Grand Canyon National Park, Arizona (© Ben Connor)
p.20 The border of Montana and Wyoming (WFA)
p.22 *(t)* Bow and arrows in sheath and quiver, N. Plains (© Ben Connor) (Maxwell Museum of Anthropology, University of New Mexico) *(b)* Short-handled club with agate head and wooden handle, decorated with beads and porcupine quills (© Colin Taylor)
p.23 Colorado River winding past Point Hansbrough, Grand Canyon National Park, Arizona (© Ben Connor)
p.24 Acoma turkey figurine (© Ben Connor) (Maxwell Museum of Anthropology, University of New Mexico)
p.25 Cochiti (Pueblo) storyteller figurine (© Ben Connor) (Maxwell Museum of Anthropology, University of New Mexico)
p.26 Hopi plate painted with kachina mask (© Ben Connor) (Maxwell Museum of Anthropology, University of New Mexico)
p.29 Hopi kachina doll (© Ben Connor) (Maxwell Museum of Anthropology, University of New Mexico)
p.30 Jemez (Pueblo) storyteller figurine (© Ben Connor) (Maxwell Museum of Anthropology, University of New Mexico)
p.31 Plains Indian beaded buckskin pouch in the form of a turtle (R L Anderson Coll., Plains Indian Museum, BBHC, Cody, Wyoming, USA/WFA)
p.32 Pawnee effigy pipe of a beaver and human head; made of Catlinite, a special red stone quarried in what is present-day Minnesota (© Colin Taylor)
p.35 Plains Indian war shield; it was believed that the carrier of the shield would be endowed with the bear's power and strength (Plains Indian Museum, BBHC, Cody, Wyoming, USA/WFA)
p.36 Plains Indian buffalo hide robe bears the characteristic Black War Bonnet design (Chandler Pohrt Coll., Plains Indian Museum, BBHC, Cody, Wyoming, USA/WFA)
p.37 Cascade Creek flowing through forest, Grand Teton National Park, Wyoming (© Ben Connor)
p.38 Inupiak (Alaska Eskimo) bow (sinew backed) and arrows (metal & bone points) (© Ben Connor) (Maxwell Museum of Anthropology, University of New Mexico)
p.40 Inupiak (Alaska Eskimo) seal carved in ivory (© Ben Connor) (Maxwell Museum of Anthropology, University of New Mexico)
p.41 Rattle in form of Raven (© Ben Connor) (Maxwell Museum of Anthropology, University of New Mexico)
pp.42–43 Hoodoos at Devil's Garden, Hole-in-the-Rock Road, Grand Staircase-Escalante National Mon., Utah (© Ben Connor)
p.44 Plains Indian 'Love Flute' used by suitors during courtship (Museum of the American Indian, Haye Foundation, New York, USA/WFA)
p.45 Saint Mary's Lake, Montana (WFA)
p.46 Dentalium shell necklace and beads with an attached disc of abalone (© Colin Taylor)
p.47 Fringed buckskin dress decorated with beadwork and cowrie shells (© Colin Taylor)
p.48 Haida wooden carved and painted bear mask (© Ben Connor) (Maxwell Museum of Anthropology, University of New Mexico)
p.49 Carved animal totem pole, Vancouver, Canada (Torquil Cramer/AKG London)
p.51 Tlingit wooden mask (© Ben Connor) (Maxwell Museum of Anthropology, University of New Mexico)
p.55 Plains Indian shield made from buffalo hide (Plains Indian Museum, BBHC, Cody, Wyoming, USA/WFA)
p.57 Tlingit raven ladle made of horn, bone and copper (Cleveland Museum of Art, USA/WFA)
p.58 Fairweather Ranges, northern British Colombia (© Ben Connor)
pp.60–61 Sioux pipe depicting the spirits of a couple and a horse (National Museum of the American Indian, New York, USA/WFA)
p.62 Men's buckskin leggings, heavily fringed and embellished with beadwork bands. The bead technique is the so called 'lazy stitch' (© Colin Taylor)
p.63 *(t)* A woven beaded headband, showing patterns of hills, mountains and birds (© Colin Taylor); *(b)* Ute beaded moccasins (© Ben Connor) (Maxwell Museum of Anthropology, University of New Mexico)
p.65 Sandstone tower rising above Escalante River, Horse Canyon, Grand Staircase-Escalante National Mon., Utah (© Ben Connor)
p.69 Pima Point looking onto Horseshoe Mesa, South Rim, Grand Canyon National Park, Arizona (© Ben Connor)
p.70 Monument Valley Navajo Tribal Park, Arizona (© Ben Connor)

pp.72–73 Colorado River and the Vermilion Cliffs at Lee's Ferry, Glen Canyon National Recreation Area, Arizona (© Ben Connor)
p.75 Plains Indian ghost-dance shirt with thunderbird design (Museum of the American Indian, Haye Foundation, New York, USA/WFA)
p.76 Thunderbird atop totem pole, Stanley Park, Vancouver, British Columbia (© Ben Connor)
p.77 Haida mask said to represent the Moon (National Museum of Man, Ottawa /WFA)
p.79 Spider Rock, Canyon de Chelly National Monument, Arizona (© Ben Connor)
p.80 Rainbow Bridge National Monument, Utah (© Ben Connor)
p.85 Tlingit woven basket with face (© Ben Connor) (Maxwell Museum of Anthropology, University of New Mexico)
p.86 A ceremonial float of a salmon carved from cedarwood, Northwest coast (© Colin Taylor)
p.89 Inuit seal carved in soapstone (© Ben Connor) (Maxwell Museum of Anthropology, University of New Mexico)
p.91 Mississippian Southern Cult shell disc incised with spider, c. 1000 AD (Field Museum of Natural History, Chicago, USA/WFA)
p.92 Plains Indian beaded buckskin pouch in the form of a snake (R L Anderson Coll., Plains Indian Museum, BBHC, Cody, Wyoming, USA/WFA)
p.93 Ceremonial tomahawk (© Ben Connor) (Maxwell Museum of Anthropology, University of New Mexico)
p.95 Tlingit prow ornament used by the Raven division at Klukwan, the largest of the Chilkat Tlingit villages (Field Museum of Natural History, Chicago, USA/WFA
p.96 Makah basket purse with whale hunt design (© Ben Connor) (Maxwell Museum of Anthropology, University of New Mexico)
pp.98–99 Shiprock, New Mexico (© Ben Connor)
p.100 Dried corn cobs (© Ben Connor)
p.101 Maize fields, Bluff, Utah (© Ben Connor)
p.102 Oglala (Lakota) stone peace pipe (© Ben Connor) (Maxwell Museum of Anthropology, University of New Mexico)
p.104 Hidatsa buffalo robe with the characteristic 'box and border' design of a woman's garment (Hassrich Collection, Plains Indian Museum, BBHC, Cody, Wyoming, USA/WFA)
p.107 Navajo sandpainting (© Ben Connor) (Maxwell Museum of Anthropology, University of New Mexico)
p.109 Owachomo Bridge, Natural Bridges National Monument, Utah (© Ben Connor)
p.110 Navajo sandpainting (© Ben Connor) (Maxwell Museum of Anthropology, University of New Mexico)
p.112 Hopi rattle made from gourd with painted star (© Ben Connor) (Maxwell Museum of Anthropology, University of New Mexico)
p.113 Zuni pot with deer and snake (© Ben Connor) (Maxwell Museum of Anthropology, University of New Mexico)
pp.116–117 Chief Mountain, northern Montana was sacred to the Blackfoot who would visit the area for meditation (WFA)
p.119 Sun symbol on a Sioux pipe bag worked with porcupine quills (© Colin Taylor)
p.120 Cochiti (Pueblo) painted drum (© Ben Connor) (Maxwell Museum of Anthropology, University of New Mexico)
p.121 A 'bear knife'; the handle is made from the jaw of a bear, Plains Indians (© Colin Taylor)
p.123 The Skeena River, British Columbia, Canada. In the background is the mountain of Stekya-den near Hazelton (WFA)
p.129 Plains Indian 'war' costume. The beaded bear paw design come from a dream/vision of the shirt wearer (L Larom Coll., Plains Indian Museum, BBHC, Cody, Wyoming, USA/WFA)
p.130 Plains Indian effigy of a buffalo. The buffalo was looked upon as sacred and was honoured in rituals and ceremonies (Glenbow Museum, Calgary, Alberta, USA/WFA)
pp.134–135 Monument Valley, Monument Valley Navajo Tribal Park, Arizona (© Ben Connor)
p.137 Sioux hand drum painted with a powerful horned figure, rarely depicted on artefacts (Plains Indian Museum, BBHC, Cody, Wyoming, USA/WFA)
p.139 Kwakiutl mask representing Tsonoqa, a giantess who carried off children to eat them (British Museum, London/WFA)
p.140 Kluane Ranges, Kluane National Park, Yukon Territory (© Ben Connor)
p.142 Tlingit rattle in the form of a salmon containing an effigy figure of a shaman (Mr & Mrs John A. Putnam/WFA)
p.144 A canoe decorated with patterns produced by scraping away the dark layers of bark (© Colin Taylor)
p.149 The Skeena River, British Columbia, Canada. Haida and Tsimshian territory (WFA)
p.151 Cochiti (Pueblo) storyteller figurine (© Ben Connor) (Maxwell Museum of Anthropology, University of New Mexico)
p.152 Woman's fringed deerskin dress, decorated with beadwork (© Colin Taylor)
p.155 Beaded moccasins (© Ben Connor) (Maxwell Museum of Anthropology, University of New Mexico)

Abbreviations
WFA – Werner Forman Archive

Acknowledgements
The author and publishers wish to thank Colin Taylor for his valuable advice and help.

pp.34–38 The author wishes to acknowledge the original storyteller of *The Buffalo Skin Sky*. Oral original collected by Gilliland, in *The Flood*. Billings: Montana Council for Indian Education, 1972. Retold in *Voices of Winds*, Edmonds & Clark, p.16.

pp.132–133 An extract from the writings of George Bird Grinnell, 1872.
Every effort has been made to contact copyright holders. If any omissions have been made, the publishers would welcome information regarding omissions.